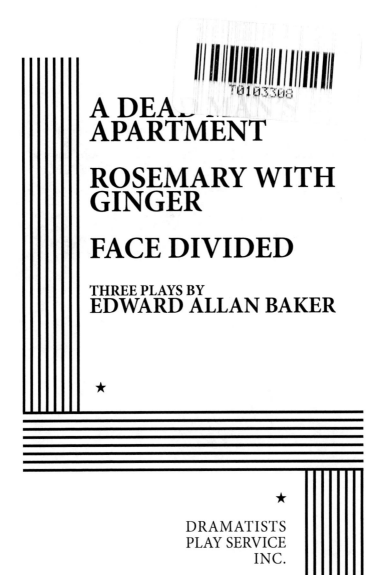

A DEAD MAN'S APARTMENT

ROSEMARY WITH GINGER

FACE DIVIDED

THREE PLAYS BY
EDWARD ALLAN BAKER

★

★

DRAMATISTS
PLAY SERVICE
INC.

NOTE ON BILLING

Anyone receiving permission to produce A DEAD MAN'S APARTMENT, ROSEMARY WITH GINGER, and/or FACE DIVIDED is required to give credit to the Author as sole and exclusive Author of the Play(s) on the title page of all programs distributed in connection with performances of the Play(s) and in all instances in which the title(s) of the Play(s) appears, including printed or digital materials for advertising, publicizing or otherwise exploiting the Play(s) and/or a production thereof. Please see your production license for font size and typeface requirements.

Be advised that there may be additional credits required in all programs and promotional material. Such language will be listed under the "Additional Billing" section of production licenses. It is the licensee's responsibility to ensure any and all required billing is included in the requisite places, per the terms of the license.

SPECIAL NOTE ON SONGS/RECORDINGS

Dramatists Play Service neither holds the rights to nor grants permission to use any songs or recordings mentioned in these Plays. Permission for performances of copyrighted songs, arrangements or recordings mentioned in these Plays is not included in our license agreement. The permission of the copyright owner(s) must be obtained for any such use. For any songs and/or recordings mentioned in these Plays, other songs, arrangements, or recordings may be substituted provided permission from the copyright owner(s) of such songs, arrangements or recordings is obtained; or songs, arrangements or recordings in the public domain may be substituted.

2

TABLE OF CONTENTS

A DEAD MAN'S
APARTMENT

This play is dedicated in the memory of James Wargowsky, a gentle man.

A DEAD MAN'S APARTMENT was produced by Showtime Networks Inc. in association with Paramount Network Television, Viacom Productions, Grammnet Productions and The Met Theatre (Risa Bramon Garcia and Jerry Levine, Producers), in Act One 95, a Festival of New One Act Plays, in Los Angeles, California, in May, 1995. It was directed by Risa Bramon Garcia; the set design was by Maggie Stewart; the costume design was by Taylor Kincaid Cheek; the lighting design was by Rand Ryan; the sound design and original music was by Ben Decter and the stage manager was Antoinette Papazian. The cast was as follows:

LONNIE .... Pruitt Taylor Vince
VALERIE-MARIE .... Brittany Murphy
NICKIE .... Amy Pietz
AL ....Jay Thomas

A DEAD MAN'S APARTMENT was produced by Ensemble Studio Theatre (Curt Dempster, Artistic Director) in New York City, in April, 1995. It was directed by Ron Stetson; the set design was by Kert Lundell; the costume design was by Lourdes Garcia; the lighting design was by Greg MacPherson; the sound design was by Jeffrey M. Taylor and the stage manager was Kelly Corona. The cast was as follows:

LONNIE .... David McConeghey
VALERIE .... Alexondra Lee
NICKIE .... Ilene Kristen
AL .... Bill Cwikowski

CHARACTERS

LONNIE (man in late 30s)
NICKIE (woman same age)
VALERIE MARIE (Nickie's daughter, 17)
AL (45ish)

PLACE

A second floor walkup in Providence, Rhode Island.

TIME

Noonish. Summer, 1995.

SETTING

Apartment is lightly furnished. A couch. Kitchen table with some chairs around it. Lamp or two. Couple of other chairs. Small table with a framed picture of Nickie and Lonnie. Pile of newspapers. Empty pizza boxes scattered about along with soda bottles, boxes of cookies, donut boxes, boxes of cereal, and some artificial flowers here and there. There's a window upstage center with a shade pulled all the way down. Door to the outside is upstage left. A phone and phone answering machine are downstage center. A horse calendar is on stage-right wall.

Pre-show music — Etta James*

* See Special Note on Songs and Recordings on copyright page.

AUTHORS NOTE

Writing A DEAD MAN'S APARTMENT was great fun for me. I just got out of its way. The writing master Ray Bradbury said: "Self-consciousness is the enemy of all art, be it acting, writing, painting, or living itself, which is the greatest art of all."

A DEAD MAN'S APARTMENT

Scene: pre-show music and lights fade to black. Pause. Lights up on Lonnie, a balding overweight man clad in workman's overalls. He dashes to the phone machine on the floor. He hits the play button and hears:

MAN'S VOICE. "You're a dead man." *(Lonnie shakes his head.)*
LONNIE. Shit ... *(He plays it again.)*
MAN'S VOICE. "You're a dead man." *(Lonnie stands up. Paces, nervously.)*
LONNIE. Shit, she's gonna know it's me, goddamn it! Uh ... *(He practices Italian-style.)* You're a dead – a man – ah. *(Doesn't like it. Again, louder.)* YOU ... ARE ... A ... DEAD – A MAN – A! *(Doesn't like it. Runs and grabs a dish-towel from the table. Covers his mouth then does it.)* You're a dead man ... *(He likes it. Reaches in his pocket for some change while rehearsing the phrase a few more times. He turns to go for the door when it suddenly opens revealing Nickie. In sunglasses, baseball cap, and a hardware-store smock. She looks at Lonnie.)*
NICKIE. Today's the day, Lonnie. I can't do this anymore. I can't pretend that I believe somethin' that I don't 'cause a the kids yunno, they been in the way an' I – I don't want to be with you anymore, next to you, callin' you or or ironin' your shirts or cookin' your meals. *(She has backed Lonnie to the couch. She rips off her hat, glasses, and smock. Drops her pocketbook.)* I'm at a place that is kinda hard to explain' but I know it's the end of something and I want to get out before I reach forty, okay? I feel sick inside 'cause of it every day an' an' at night I sit on the edge of the bed an' I see your shape an' I hear you snorin' an' I grab my Saint Jude Medal an' I pray for strength, for help, an' I say "GET ME THE FUCK OUT OF THIS MESS!" I – I say it with tears in my eyes an' I say it

11

really pissed off an I say it every night. I – I have to say it'd be easier in a way if you hit me an' the kids but you never did an' you always get your ass outta bed in the mornin' to go to work to pay the bills ... it's just that um ... that I don't feel anything deep for you AND I'M SO FUCKIN' BORED I COULD DIE, DO YOU UNDERSTAND?! *(Lonnie stirs to get up. She waves him off.)* Wait wait ... *(Beat.)* Where are we goin'? I'm afraid and I just want to snap my fingers an' go foward five years or back twenty. I for a long time have felt my weddin' ring is around my neck an' gettin' tighter an' tighter an' ...

LONNIE.   *(Rises.)* Okay Nickie, I ...

NICKIE.   LET ME GO! JUST LET ME GO! Please say "it's all right, I understand, have a good life, good luck, and good bye." An then just go. Walk away. No no tears. No anger. No hurt feelings. Just ... walk ... away ... from me ... *(Lonnie waits. She nods. He rises to where she was standing. She sits on the couch. He begins to get out of his overalls and struggles in doing so.)*

LONNIE.   *(After a nervous moment.)* I'm ... goin' to leave you ...

NICKIE.   *(Waits a beat.)* Uh-huh ... and ... why are ...

LONNIE.   'Cause I've thought it out an' I'm ...

NICKIE.   You're ...

LONNIE.   Leavin'. I thought it out ...

NICKIE.   What? That's it?

LONNIE.   *(Holds his hand up.)* This isn't as easy for me as as it was for you ...

NICKIE.   You're right, you're right ...

LONNIE.   *(Continues.)* Uh ... I – I want to get out of this before I'm forty an' I – I'm so sick of your shape ... in the in our bed, an' it makes me sick inside an' you're good with the kids an' an'cookin' an' you do get up, you know, in the mornin' an' uh I uh you you do get up, you know in the mornin' ... *(Lonnie finally steps out of his overalls in the L. area revealing him in Bermuda shorts, flowery shirt, black socks and sandals.)* An uh you you never hit me an' I'd say that's a good thing an' ...

NICKIE.   *(Suspicious.)* Lonnie ...

LONNIE.   *(Continuing.)* And if I had a Saint medal, I would scream to its face "GET ME THE FUCK ..."

NICKIE. *(Stands.)* LONNIE! *(Lonnie looks at her.)* Are you havin' doubts?

LONNIE. *(Lightens up.)* Oh, oh, you're havin' doubts?

NICKIE. NO! I love you Lonnie!

LONNIE. And I love you Nickie! *(They run into each others arms and kiss passionately.)*

NICKIE. Oh God please don't have doubts ...

LONNIE. The way you ended tellin' your husband uh, "say it's all right, I understand, have a good life ..."

NICKIE. "... good luck an' goodbye an' then just go, just leave me, no tears, no ..."

LONNIE. It won't happen that way.

NICKIE. It might.

LONNIE. If that happened ...

NICKIE. I know it won't be easy but ...

LONNIE. If that happened ...

NICKIE. But it might if ...

LONNIE. If that happened ...

NICKIE. If he believes I'm ... oh I'm sorry. Finish. Finish. "If that happened ..."

LONNIE. If that happened, maybe what we have wouldn't be as deep.

NICKIE. "If that happened, maybe what we have wouldn't be as deep."

LONNIE. You know what I'm sayin'?

NICKIE. "If that happened, maybe what we ..."

LONNIE. Nickie, there's somethin' else ...

NICKIE. *(Pulls away from Lonnie.)* You're not goin' to leave her, are you?

LONNIE. Listen to me. I know that leavin' my wife an' kids is the right thing to do, shit, I felt that the first time I saw you behind the counter of the hardware store but ... *(He takes a breath, holds her steady.)* Somebody wants to take me out.

NICKIE. On a date?

LONNIE. No! Take me out like ... kill!

NICKIE. Who would want to kill you?

LONNIE. When I got here today I – I saw the light on the

13

machine flashing an' ... well just listen ... *(He gets on his knees. He plays it for her.)*

MAN'S VOICE. "You're a dead man." *(Nickie screams out loud. He plays it again.)* "You're a dead man." *(Nickie gets on her knees next to Lonnie.)*

NICKIE. *(Whispers.)* Who the hell could that be?

LONNIE. *(Whispers.)* Is it your husband?

NICKIE. *(Whispers.)* I ... do you think it's your wife?

LONNIE. *(Harsh whisper back.)* How the hell could it be my wife?

NICKIE. Maybe she had someone do it.

LONNIE. Could be the same for you.

NICKIE. "Could be the same for you."

LONNIE. Your husband had someone do it.

NICKIE. "Your husband had ..."

LONNIE. *(Stands, upset.)* For chrissakes Nickie, is it or isn't it?!

NICKIE. *(Hurt.)* Lonnie ... that's the first time you ever yelled at me.

LONNIE. I'm sorry. Just a little nervous.... Uh, death bothers me. *(Nickie stands and hugs him.)*

NICKIE. I don't want nothin' to happen to you, oh my god ...

LONNIE. I know you don't.

NICKIE. If you die ...

LONNIE. You'd die.

NICKIE. *(Beat.)* I don't know, I got kids, Hon.

LONNIE. *(Turns away.)* Right – right.

NICKIE. Part a me would die, though.

LONNIE. Yup – yup.

NICKIE. *(Goes to Lonnie.)* Would you die if I died?

LONNIE. I got kids too.

NICKIE. That's what I'm sayin'.

LONNIE. Same thing, uh part a me would die.

NICKIE. That's what I'm sayin' so don't be hurt, okay? *(They embrace warmly.)*

LONNIE. Do you think it's your husband?

NICKIE. God, no, it couldn't be because how would he

know? *(She moves from Lonnie, thinking.)* Unless …

LONNIE. Unless what?

NICKIE. *(Talking to herself.)* Unless she was so mad at me an' decided to tell …

LONNIE. *(Cuts Nickie off.)* Who are you talkin' about?!

NICKIE. Valerie!

LONNIE. You told your daughter about us?! *(Nickie goes to the door and swings it open, yells out.)*

NICKIE. VALERIE MARIE! *(Lonnie runs to Nickie.)*

LONNIE. Wait a minute, wait a minute! *(He closes door.)*

NICKIE. Lonnie, it's all right. Me an' her, we're like girl-friends … *(She reopens the door, yells out.)* GET UP HERE!

VALERIE. *(From offstage.)* ALL RIGHT!

LONNIE. *(Closes door.)* This is the same girl who tried to kill herself three times?!

NICKIE. Four if you count the toilet bowl incident but …

LONNIE. *(Blocks door.)* I'm very nervous about this …

NICKIE. *(Gets close to Lonnie.)* You love me, don't you? *(Lonnie nods.)* Then move from the door, c'mon, we're on a lunch break. *(Sudden knocking at the door. Lonnie tenses up.)*

LONNIE. Maybe I'll just leave an' you play the message for her without me bein' here an' that way if … *(Nickie grabs Lonnie's face and kisses him, madly, then yanks him from the door. She throws it open and is face to face with Valerie.)*

NICKIE. Did you tell your father about me an' Lonnie?!

VALERIE. *(Dryly.)* Jesus Christ, Ma, is this him?

LONNIE. *(From across the room.)* Hi.

NICKIE. *(Closes door.)* Lonnie, Valerie. Valerie, Lonnie. *(Valerie is clad in baggy jeans, a flannel shirt over a tee-shirt, and a baseball cap worn backwards. She stares at Lonnie.)*

VALERIE. You a chef or somethin'?

NICKIE. I told you he's a mechanic.

VALERIE. He looks like a chef.

NICKIE. He works on firetrucks.

VALERIE. He looks like a chef.

LONNIE. I work on firetrucks.

NICKIE. *(By the phone machine.)* Get over here, Valerie.

VALERIE. *(Eyes on Lonnie.)* So you're the guy with the "big heart."

NICKIE.   Listen to this an' tell me who it is. *(She plays message.)*

MAN'S VOICE.   "You're a dead man."

NICKIE.   Is that your father?

VALERIE.   I can't tell.

NICKIE.   Get on the floor an' listen again. *(Valerie does. Message replayed.)*

MAN'S VOICE.   "You're a dead man."

VALERIE.   Ma, I can't tell ...

NICKIE.   Listen again, closer this time ... *(She holds Valerie's head down to the machine.)*

MAN'S VOICE.   "You're a dead man."

VALERIE.   No idea. *(Nickie releases her.)*

LONNIE.   Uh, forget the message for a sec an' let me ask you a question if I can.... Did you speak to your father about your mother and I?

VALERIE.   Whadda you, retarded?

NICKIE.   *(Hits Valerie.)* Watch your mouth!

VALERIE.   He asked me a retarded question!

NICKIE.   It's not a ...

LONNIE.   *(Interrupts.)* Okay, okay, so you didn't?

NICKIE.   You didn't, right?

VALERIE.   *(Stands.)* Me an' him don't talk. Don't know how to.

NICKIE.   *(To Lonnie.)* It's true. They don't.

VALERIE.   Once a year on my birthday he gives me a real weak hug.

NICKIE.   Well next year on your birthday you're gonna get a hug from the king-of-hugs, right Lonnie? *(Gestures to Lonnie.)* C'mon, give her a hug, c'mon ...

VALERIE.   *(Backs away.)* Ma, I don't think so ... *(Nickie brings her to Lonnie.)*

NICKIE.   Hug, hug, feel what a real hug is like.

LONNIE.   *(To Valerie.)* It's okay, you don't have to ...

NICKIE.   C'mon.

VALERIE.   Some other time.

LONNIE.   Sure.

NICKIE. No, now!

LONNIE. Nickie ...

NICKIE. Hug ... hug, hug, HUG!

LONNIE. Okay, all right ... *(They hug. Nickie stands back to admire.)*

NICKIE. This is soooo nice.

LONNIE. We done?

NICKIE. Huh, Val? Somethin', isn't it?

LONNIE. *(Uncomfortable.)* Okay Val ... you can ... uh Val? *(Valerie has tightened her grip on him.)*

NICKIE. You gotta let go Honey, it's not your birthday, c'mon ...

LONNIE. C'mon Val, we got other things to uh do so ...

NICKIE. *(Pulling at Valerie.)* You gotta let him go ... *(More pulling.)* Valerie ... let ... the ... man ... go!

LONNIE. *(Struggles.)* C'mon Valerie ...

NICKIE. *(Steps back.)* Oh Christ! Bang her up against the wall!

LONNIE. I'm not gonna bang her up against the ...

NICKIE. God I love you! You're so sensitive ... *(She kisses Lonnie passionately then tries again to pry Valerie loose from Lonnie.)* Valerie Marie, stop actin' like a pit-bull an' let the man go! *(Valerie hangs tighter.)*

LONNIE. Val? Can you hear us? Can she hear us?

NICKIE. *(Again, backs off.)* Oh I can't believe this. I am so embarrassed. Uh I'll be right back. *(She dashes to the door. Lonnie follows her with Valerie attached to him.)*

LONNIE. Where the hell you goin'?!

NICKIE. *(At the door, opens it.)* I gotta get my brother ... *(She is gone.)*

LONNIE. No! *(He yells out the door.)* I'll bang her up against the wall! Nickie! *(Silence. He closes the door.)* Great. *(He moves deeper into the flat with Valerie attached to him.)* You want somethin'? Doughnut? Soda?

VALERIE. *(Muffled.)* Diet?

LONNIE. Yeah.

VALERIE. I hate diet soda. *(Lonnie paces some.)*

LONNIE. You really should let go now.

VALERIE. I don't want to.

LONNIE.   Why?

VALERIE.   I don't know why.

LONNIE.   You don't know why?

VALERIE.   I don't know why. *(Lonnie paces around the room with Valerie attached to him.)*

LONNIE.   Uh okay but just a little thing that kinda bothers me ... *(He ambles over to the window and peers out.)* I'm a little nervous today about a lot of things an' added to that as of right now is your Uncle comin' in here an' seein' you attached to me. I don't think it's how we should first meet, you know what I'm sayin'?

VALERIE.   *(Suddenly lets him go.)* I'm not stupid!

LONNIE.   *(Relieved.)* And I'm not sayin' you are. You look very stable to me.

VALERIE.   *(She takes a step closer to Lonnie and screams at him, insanely.)* You're just like everybody else! Just like those assholes in school sayin' shit like "don't fuck, don't smoke, don't wear hats, don't drink and drive!" Don't – don't don't! Meanwhile ... *(She pauses, looks at him.)* You listening to me? *(He nods.)* Meanwhile, the TV and magazines are sayin' drink! Smoke! Fuck! Drive this car! Image is everything!" *(Valerie is pacing like a maddened animal, fists clenched. Lonnie eyes her.)* I am so sick of it, so so so sick of being pulled an' pulled pulled! I am so so sick ... of ... it! *(She scoops up a bag of Oreo cookies from the table then plops down on the couch. Lonnie inches toward her. She opens a cookie and begins eating the icing, slowly.)* After I quit school I was watchin' talk shows like oh probly uh maybe I don't know ... ten, twelve a day 'cause I had the house to myself ... *(Eats the cookie.)* Then ... I got so fuckin' bored at these these assholes on TV that I ... MISS STUPID ... decided I would look an' look for stuff my parents had hidden away from me an' me MISS STUPID found these notebooks a my mothers an' I, man, I hit the jackpot, lemme tell ya ... *(Leans forward.)* I know all about you.

LONNIE.   What do you know a...?

VALERIE.   I know about the cyst you had on your ...

LONNIE.   *(Quickly.)* It was a birthmark.

VALERIE.   I know you hate mushrooms. Shellfish. Ham.

18

Chi-chi beans. I know you think your death will come by drowning.

LONNIE. That's changin' but um ...

VALERIE. I know you cried the time my mother gave you the first backrub you ever had.

LONNIE. *(Worriedly.)* You didn't show your father those notebooks, did you? I mean I don't know you so I have to ...

VALERIE. *(Snaps.)* Fuck him! As soon as I got tits we stopped talkin'. He's nothin' but a shadow who can piss an' I don't give him the time of day. *(She gets on the floor next to the machine. She plays the message.)*

MAN'S VOICE. "You're a dead man."

VALERIE. Could be him.

LONNIE. Uh yeah could be him, but listen ...

VALERIE. Has reason.

LONNIE. Uh-huh yeah, um ...

VALERIE. But I don't know.

LONNIE. But you said he "has reason."

VALERIE. *(Looks up at Lonnie.)* Could be him.

LONNIE. Okay okay, lemme ask you this, uh, has he ever ... has he ever hurt anyone before?

VALERIE. "Has he ever ... has he ever hurt anyone before?"

LONNIE. You know, gettin' jealous and hit. Shoot. Beat up.

VALERIE. Have you?

LONNIE. No.

VALERIE. You fuckin' whacked your son one time, didn't you?

LONNIE. What? How did you know that?

VALERIE. *(Coyly.)* He told me.

LONNIE. *(Aghast.)* You talked with my son?! *(Door bursts open. Nickie re-enters with Brother Al right behind her.)*

NICKIE. Oh good, she's off a him!

AL. This him?

NICKIE. Al, Lonnie. Lonnie, Al. *(An exchange of vague nods. Nickie goes to Lonnie.)* No need to be nervous, Lonnie. Al only wants what's good for me.

LONNIE. Good good, that's good. *(Al is a tough-looking man clad in jeans, tight tee-shirt that display his muscles. He wears work*

19

boots. He is eating a sandwich and carrying a metal lunch box. He is fixed on Lonnie as Nickie bends to the phone machine.)

NICKIE. Ready Al?

AL. Hit it. *(She does.)*

MAN'S VOICE. "You're a dead man."

NICKIE. Did you hear it, Al?

AL. *(Looking at Lonnie.)* I was chewin' too loud. Hit it again. *(Nickie does.)*

MAN'S VOICE. "You're a dead man."

LONNIE. Boy do I hate hearin' that.

AL. Don't blame ya ...

NICKIE. What do you think, Al?

AL. I think someone's out to kill him.

NICKIE. No shit, Al, do you know who it is?

AL. I don't give a shit who it is, they're not tryin' to kill me ... *(Looks at Lonnie.)* But it it'd scare me, I know that. *(Lonnie goes to Nickie, pulls her aside to talk.)*

LONNIE. Okay okay then let's ... Nickie, let's just back off for today or for a coupla days an' then we'll ...

NICKIE. NO! You can't do this to me!

LONNIE. Listen, just until ...

NICKIE. No!

LONNIE. ... until we let things settle down ...

NICKIE. 'Cause you'll go back to her an' probly pick another hardware store to go to an' that'll be it!

LONNIE. Calm down, calm down ... *(Al snaps his fingers to get Valerie with him and makes to the door.)*

AL. Let's go, Nickie ...

NICKIE. No! Lonnie, tell Al what you told me that time we was flyin' kites ...

VALERIE. *(Smugly.)* "I never felt this strong for anybody in my whole life."

NICKIE. *(Stunned.)* How did you know that?

VALERIE. Your notebooks, Ma.

AL. *(Bemusedly.)* You two was flyin' kites?

VALERIE. "I want a man to kiss me forever."

NICKIE. *(Goes to Valerie.)* Two can play this game.

VALERIE. "I want a man to wake me up just to hold me

20

tight."

NICKIE. "I love it when Greg looks at my chest!"

VALERIE. *(Stunned.)* You read my diary?!

NICKIE. "I'd sleep with Larry in two seconds if he asked!"

VALERIE. "I feel so hungry for somethin' I can't explain!"

NICKIE. *(Face to face with Valerie.)* "I wanna scream out I ITCH SO BAD I CAN'T SLEEP!"

AL. HEY! SEPARATE! *(The girls part quickly. Slight pause.)*

LONNIE. *(Finally.)* So look ... we're all on a lunch break here an' – an' ... *(He inches his way along the back wall toward the door.)* Time's runnin' out so why don't we go back to work an' ...

AL. *(In Lonnie's way.)* You still thinkin' a breakin' with your wife tonight?

NICKIE. *(Goes to Lonnie.)* Yes he is! Tell him Lonnie! Say yes – you – are!

LONNIE. Well so much has happened and I ... *(Nickie pushes him up against the wall.)*

NICKIE. I need you. I need your life in my life, oh please don't back from our promises ...

AL. Anythin' the two of you had is by the boards 'cause the man is scared a losin' his wife ...

LONNIE. Life.

AL. What?

LONNIE. You said "scared a losin' his wife" but you meant life.

NICKIE. Oh God Lonnie, are you ascared a losin' your wife?

LONNIE. Life!

AL. *(Closes in on Lonnie.)* But if you really loved Nickie, you'd do right by her, right or wrong?

NICKIE. And he's goin' to, right Lonnie?

VALERIE. God Ma, stop slobbering.

AL. Let the man speak. *(All look at Lonnie.)*

LONNIE. *(After a beat.)* I do ... I do love Nickie. We've had some fun.

AL. Flyin' kites ... *(Lonnie moves to the back of the couch, looks down at Nickie who is seated.)*

LONNIE. Uh, eating out.

VALERIE. Shitload a that I bet. *(Nickie makes a move to go at Valerie but Lonnie holds her shoulders.)*

AL. *(Moves in on Lonnie.)* So basic sneaking around, cheatin', screwin' around with another man's wife, tellin' her things you can't tell your wife an' doin' things you don't do with your wife an' an' ... *(Lonnie is backing from Al, Al stalks him while speaking.)* You take your wife to the show? Out to eat?

LONNIE. No. I used to.

AL. An' your wife's a housewife, right Val?

VALERIE. Yup.

AL. An' Nickie she's givin' you a a what? A glow kinda in your gut? A feelin' that gets you through a day? It makes bein' next to your wife uh harder or easier?

LONNIE. Little a both but listen ...

AL. No you listen! There are families involved! Kids. Piture albums. Mamentoes. In-laws. Bank accounts. Kids. You take your boys fishin'?

LONNIE. *(Still backing up.)* What?

AL. Bowlin'?

LONNIE. No, I ...

AL. Ball games?

LONNIE. Uh no ...

AL. Two boys, right? Right, Val?

VALERIE. *(Enjoying this.)* Ten and sixteen.

AL. You go to church?

NICKIE. I love you Lonnie ...

LONNIE. *(To Al.)* No I ...

VALERIE. *(Right behind Al.)* His son says he listens to tapes um somethin' like "unlocking your inner doorknob."

LONNIE. When did you talk to my son?

VALERIE. Last week.

LONNIE. Did you know this Nickie?

NICKIE. *(From the couch.)* I didn't think it would hurt.

LONNIE. We had an' agreement not to tell anybody about us!

NICKIE. Lonnie Hon, it's been so nice I couldn't keep it in.

AL. So okay you're listening to tapes. Uh, Val tells me your son says you're moody, sorta lazy, like to smoke grass in the basement.

VALERIE.   Can't fix anythin' but cars an' wanders winda to winda.

AL.   No shit?

VALERIE.   Plays gospel music real loud and cries.

AL.   *(To Lonnie.)* That true? *(He and Valerie have Lonnie cornered in U.R. corner.)*

LONNIE.   I don't believe this ...

AL.   Hey pal, you started this! An' I gotta know if you got the insides to go through life with my sista. That fair soundin' to you or do you got a problem with me?

NICKIE.   Be careful, Lonnie ... *(Lonnie backs further into the corner.)*

LONNIE.   No, I do have a problem with you. I have a problem now that I know my son was talked to an' an' I got a problem with the surprise of you an' an' Valerie bein' here today an' ...

VALERIE.   Don't forget the death threat.

LONNIE.   An that gospel music thing happened one time!

AL.   Can't forget someone's on to you. *(Valerie pulls Al to the side to talk with him.)*

VALERIE.   His son says that he disappears to the fuckin' basement when somethin' goes wrong or somethin' like "when he feels cornered." *(Again Lonnie is trying to inch his way to the door. Nickie notices and runs to block the doorway.)*

NICKIE.   Tell 'em Lonnie that we're goin' to a place that'll have no basement an' tell 'em you're gonna change with me an' you'll be different, c'mon, tell 'em ... *(Pause. Lonnie is motionless.)* C'mon ... tell 'em ... *(Lonnie remains unblinkingly still. Nickie rubs his face in a loving manner.)* Okay then, let's tell 'em together, okay? You wanna do that? Tell 'em together? *(Lonnie nods, barely. Al and Valerie laugh and move to sit and eat together. Nickie coaxes Lonnie, pulling him toward Al and Valerie.)*

NICKIE.   Nickie and I we ... we ...

LONNIE.   *(Softly.)* Take walks ...

NICKIE.   Holdin' hands an' ...

LONNIE.   An she loves lookin' at horses. So we do that ...

NICKIE.   An we eat ...

LONNIE and NICKIE.   Clamcakes ...

LONNIE.   *(Gaining energy.)* On the rocks a Narragansett ...

NICKIE.   Not lettin' the spray a the waves bother us ... and we talk ...

LONNIE.   To each other ...

NICKIE and LONNIE.   Every day ...

LONNIE.   An then gettin' a place hidden away an' an' the phone an' machine was to have in case one of us couldn't get here ...

NICKIE.   'Cause a some family thing ...

LONNIE.   We decided to do that ... *(Al and Valerie stare at them in quiet disbelief.)*

NICKIE.   An then we set a date to tell our, which is today an' uh ...

LONNIE.   *(Cuts in.)* An then this message kinda made me look, uh think at what we intend to do uh real hard an' ... uh ... *(Nickie whispers something to him. Moves behind Valerie and Al.)* Uh ... I went with Nickie to her fathers grave an' I stood there in the rain' an' watched her cry an' bend to smooth the stone with her hand ... *(Awkward silence for a beat. Al is waiting.)*

NICKIE.   An you said ... when I came back to the car, you said ...

LONNIE.   Oh-oh. I said it looked like she was rubbin' his face ...

NICKIE.   *(Leans to Al and Valerie.)* Isn't that nice? *(Nothing from Al and Valerie.)*

LONNIE.   I felt something for her in a place I never been to before an' ... *(Lowers his head. He begins to cry, softly.)*

VALERIE.   You never been to a graveyard?

NICKIE.   *(Moved.)* Oh Lonnie ... *(She is comforting Lonnie.)*

AL.   Whoa – whoa is he ballin'?

NICKIE.   I told you he was sensitive.

AL.   *(To Valerie.)* Is he fuckin' ballin'?!

VALERIE.   *(Goes to look.)* He's fuckin' ballin'.

AL.   *(Stands up.)* Don't let me see you ballin', pal, 'cause I'll whack you!

NICKIE.   Cut it out Al!

AL. An' worse than that is a woman goin' "oh he's so sensitive, I think I'll love him!"

NICKIE. He's all upset 'cause a that ... *(Gestures to phone machine. Lonnie is trying to recover.)*

AL. This is it?! *(Nickie is wiping Lonnie's face with a Kleenex.)*

NICKIE. Take a breath, Lon-hon ...

AL. *(Pacing.)* This guy is what you want?! So you can go an' fly kites an' cry together?! This is what blowin' my lunch hour is been about?! I thought I was comin' to meet a man!

NICKIE. You're not seein' the real Lonnie! *(She sits Lonnie down on the couch.)*

AL. *(Goes at Lonnie.)* Whadda you goin' to do when her son gets outta drug re-hab an' needs you? Whadda you goin' to do when Val here comes screamin' to you for answers? You goin' to start cryin'? You goin' to say "the hell with this" an' go back to your wife? You goin' to give 'em the wrong answers?!

NICKIE. *(Gets between Al and Lonnie.)* Stop it Al! You don't understand, he's more than what you're gettin' today on account a that damn message an' ...

AL. *(Moves by Nickie.)* Do you think leavin' your wife for Nickie is goin' to make you smart all of a sudden?

NICKIE. He's not lookin' to be smart!

VALERIE. "He's not lookin' to be smart!" *(Lonnie is feeling the bombardment as he slouches down on the couch.)*

LONNIE. Stop ... look ... just just ... please just ... *(Al has had enough. He picks up his lunch box and makes for the door. Nickie runs and stops him before he can exit.)*

NICKIE. Listen to me, Al, this is the man I – I want an' I know you're seein' just the outside an' an' ... look at me Al! *(Al does.)* I need him ... I'm so afraid of ... of turnin' into a a dried up woman, like Ma, yunno?

AL. *(Points a finger at her.)* Hey! *(He attempts to leave but Nickie swipes his lunch box.)*

NICKIE. Look at me Al an' I'm askin' you to go deep down an' an' understand why I need Lonnie an' ... an' then, let us go. Let me feel a man's hand on my face again. Look at me Al ... *(He does.)* I'm so tired a standin' still. I – I want the

25

warmth … Lonnie's warmth to move me inside to bein' happy. *(She hands him back his lunch box then rejoins Lonnie on the couch. They hold hands. Al takes a full moment to eye the both of them on the couch. He looks straight at Lonnie.)*

AL.   Is this a dick thing?

LONNIE.   What?

AL.   This has got to be a dick thing, right?

NICKIE.   We haven't even had sex!

AL.   *(To Lonnie.)* True?

LONNIE.   True.

VALERIE.   Wonda if the person who wants to kill ya knows that?

LONNIE.   *(To Al.)* All we been doin' in here is is kissin' on the couch an' talkin' about uh life an' dreamin' a bein' together, of of another life together!

AL.   Oh that sounds like alotta fun … *(Al walks away from them. He is thinking. All wait for his next word. Finally:)* Val, do your thing?

LONNIE.   What? What thing?

AL.   *(To Valerie.)* Kinda like the shit you did to me last week.

NICKIE.   *(Rises from the couch.)* Oh shit …

VALERIE.   The uh I-don't-wanna-live-no-more or the-bangin'-the-head-up-against the-wall?

AL.   Go with the I-don't-wanna-live-no-more. *(Valerie starts to hyperventilate, getting ready.)*

NICKIE.   Do your best Lonnie.

LONNIE.   Best at what?!

AL.   *(Instructs Lonnie.)* Okay so now you're in the parlor…. An' an' say you an' Nickie are a "thing" now an' an' Val comes outta somewhere all upset an' has no one else to go to but you …

LONNIE.   *(To Nickie.)* Why did you bring them here?!

AL.   *(Walking away.)* You can't cash in nothin' and get somethin'!

LONNIE.   What the hell does that mean?!

NICKIE.   I love you Lonnie …

LONNIE.   Then why are you doin' this?!

VALERIE.   *(Next to Al.)* Can I start now?

NICKIE. *(Rushes to Lonnie on the couch.)* Listen to me, you can do it. Prove to them we can and will be happy before our lunch break is up. *(Al moves Nickie away from Lonnie just as Valerie jumps on the couch then leans into Lonnie's face.)*

VALERIE. I want to die! I can't see any reason to get up anymore!

LONNIE. Nickie, I'm hurtin' ...

VALERIE. My mother just says "do what I say!" An my father says "get off the couch I gotta lay down" an' every day is the same an' I ...

LONNIE. Nickie ...

VALERIE. Maybe people will feel for me when I'm dead — THE PAIN OF LIVIN' WILL BE OVER —

LONNIE. Nickie, why can't we just go on the way we been goin'?!

NICKIE. *(Goes to Lonnie.)* Lonnie, your face is flushed ... *(To Al.)* I never seen that before.

AL. *(Bends to Lonnie.)* Never mind her, what are you goin' to say to Val?!

VALERIE. *(Still atop Lonnie.)* A knife in my heart, a rope around my neck ...

LONNIE. I have no idea what you're doin'!

VALERIE. *(Looks at Al.)* Should I stop?

AL. No, keep goin' Val!

NICKIE. Start fightin' Lonnie Honey!

VALERIE. I don't wanna live oh stepfather an' I need to hear from somebody on why I should, okay?!

LONNIE. *(In her face.)* Well, FUCK YOU, okay?!

VALERIE. Gimme a reason oh stepfather for seein' the sun come up tammara! *(Lonnie struggles to get off the couch.)*

LONNIE. Oh for Chrissakes ... *(He turns around to face Valerie who is standing on the couch.)*

VALERIE. I – I ... look I bit my wrist open an' it's bleedin', hurry I'm bleedin' bad ...

LONNIE. You're not bleedin'!

VALERIE. *(Holds out her wrist.)* My blood ... it's drippin' on your feet, it's gettin' ... I'm gettin' ... I'm feelin' so so weak ... *(She falls into Lonnie's arms. Lonnie lays her down on the couch.)*

LONNIE.   I don't know what to tell you ... I got through it. We all get through it. You do what you have to do and you get through it an' yeah yeah most of it sucks but you push on, push on past the beatin's an' the bein' ignored an' push past no one there to hold you an' you fuckin' push on past when you think you don't matta an' nothin' matters an' there's no peace in anybody's fuckin' house! For Chrissakes people dyin' for gettin' laid an' other people dyin' 'cause they can't get laid an' you kids ... you goddamn kids nowadays ... you want all the answers like right away! "Gimme an answer or I'll kill myself!" WELL FUCK YOU! You don't think we had ... we adults had pain when we was growin' up?! For Chrissakes WAKE THE FUCK UP an' be thankful you got a roof over ya head an' food on the table an' a bed to wallow over your bullshit in! Be thankful for the malls you hang out in an' for the stupid clothes ya wear an' the teachers you insult and hate! *(Valerie gets up from the couch to cross the room and is stopped by Lonnie who spins her around to face him. He shakes her.)* Just know that all this will pass, god damn it, all ... of ... this ... will ... pass! *(Silence. Valerie walks to Nickie.)*

VALERIE.   *(Looks at Lonnie.)* Oh yeah, I really wanna live now.

LONNIE.   *(Turns around to Al.)* Don't you agree? I mean these kids, they gotta be told an' I'm sick a them thinkin' they can say whatever they want an' ... *(Al presses down on the answering machine with his foot.)*

MAN'S VOICE.   "You're a dead man." *(A slight pause. Lonnie turns to Nickie.)*

LONNIE.   Nickie, say somethin', tell 'em our love is in this apartment an' how much we shared ...

VALERIE.   Ma, he's the worst one of the whole bunch. *(Lonnie's face drops.)*

LONNIE.   What? What did you say?

AL.   Lon-man, it's all over.

LONNIE.   *(Angrily.)* Hey, technically speaking, this is our apartment an' I could kick your ass outta here or call the cops!

AL.   *(Gets closer to Lonnie.)* I own this building, pal! So technically speaking I'm your landlord an' I let Nickie use it when

28

she thinks someone like you is the ONE to save her. Shit, I could name five, six guys in the past ...

NICKIE. Don't ...

AL. I won't Honey ... *(Nickie crosses to the U. table to get the picture of she and Lonnie.)*

NICKIE. Poor Lonnie ... *(She removes the photo.)*

AL. It's all over between you an' my sista.

LONNIE. I'm not gonna let this happen.

AL. What are you gonna do? *(Lonnie runs to Nickie and picks her up, holds her in a bear hug.)*

LONNIE. Oh god Nickie, it's been so nice that no matta what was goin' on in my home life, I always knew I had this an' an' you ...

AL. Let her go ...

NICKIE. *(Struggling.)* Lonnie, let me go ...

LONNIE. What we had was fine 'til ...

AL. *(Pulling at Lonnie.)* It's over, let her go!

NICKIE. I – I can't breathe ... *(Valerie is helping Al to get Lonnie to release Nickie.)*

LONNIE. I need you to hold me on Tuesdays an' Thursdays an' an' let's add on Sundays, okay?!!

AL. *(Pulls harder at Lonnie.)* C'mon, that's enough ... let go ...

NICKIE. *(Barely audible.)* I ... please ... Lon ... *(Al gets close to Lonnie's ear.)*

AL. I killed a man in this apartment! *(Lonnie looks at Nickie. She nods. Lonnie puts Nickie down, releases her.)* A man who was screwin' my wife. Name un-important. I stabbed him beyond repair. *(Nickie is at the table with Valerie, recovering. Takes out her makeup.)* I watched them from the building across the street. I saw him massaging her breasts, the same breasts I kissed when she was seventeen ... those were my breasts! His tongue in her ear, that was MY ear! She was doin' it with this bum afta she found out I screwed a friend a hers which I could not help by the way, I mean I spent so much time fantasizin' about her that the first time alone with her I ... well it was easy to get started 'cause I had done her so many times in my head but ... uh shit, where was I goin' with this?

VALERIE. Killin' the bum.

NICKIE. "... his tongue in her ear that was my ear ..."

AL. Right. So I went nuts. I – I came runnin' over here and kicked in the door an' he turned, saw me, pulled up his fly an' ran over to the winda an' I ... I ...

NICKIE. Hurry, Al, hurry ...

AL. It happened fast an' uh funny the things ya rememba but I rememba he he smelled like her ... her smell was all over him ... Shall-la-mar ... *(Lost for a beat.)* Uh I did my time, my crime-of-passion time, an' I a course lost her, a course. She's married now to Paul Morretti ...

NICKIE. Morretti of Morretti's pizza ...

VALERIE. The one on Pontiac Avenue, that one ...

NICKIE. *(Caringly.)* Al, don't drive down there no more, you hear me?

AL. Yeah ... I uh ... my two kids I don't see no more, yunno, cut off from that an' now I protect Nickie from guys like you Lon-man. All you guys, right? All you guys who wanna be safe with somebody but got nothin' but what? Dirty laundry? You can't help her but yunno, I don't blame ya, lookit Nickie, she's beaudiful, right? She looks like she's twenty years old for Chrissakes, an' an' her heart up in her eyes an' those teeth, the smile of of niceness ... *(Nickie beams. Valerie is bored. Lonnie drained.)*

NICKIE. Al Hon, c'mon I don't wanna get fired.

AL. *(Goes to Lonnie.)* But hey, I love the thing about the tape you listen to ... the ... uh ...

VALERIE. "Unlocking your inner doorknob" but c'mon Uncle Al, let's ...

AL. *(Cuts her off.)* That's a new one, shit, betta than the mailman who said he and Nickie were lovers in a past life in uh ...

NICKIE. Mongolia.

AL. *(Laughs.)* Ain't that a winna! Fuckin' Mongolia! *(Al, Nickie and Valerie have a good laugh. When it dies down they all look to Lonnie alone on the couch. Al goes and sits next to him.)* Cheer up Lonnie, I maybe saved your life 'cause hey who knows maybe if you and Nickie say got together an' one night you an' she have a spat an' you get to feelin' a little homesick an' you circle your old house an' there's a car in the driveway you recognize an' you start to burn inside real hot in the gut an' memories from in that house start to surface yunno, holidays, birthdays, Monopoly, an' you look in the winda an' you see her sittin' there lookin' the best she's looked in years an' there's a guy on the couch next to her, an' he's smilin' an' she's smilin' ... *(He takes a moment, then:)* Are you ready to see somebody goin' afta your wife the way you been goin' afta Nickie?

LONNIE. *(Pauses a moment.)* No.

VALERIE. *(At the door.)* Good. Can we get outta here now?

NICKIE. *(Goes to Lonnie.)* So I guess this is ... *(Stops, looks to Al.)* Hey, what about the "you're a dead man" guy?

AL. Tell her Lonnie.

LONNIE. Uh ... it's me. I'm the "you're a dead man" guy.

NICKIE. You threatened your own life?!

LONNIE. I did it to stall the breakin' up with my wife 'cause I wanted to keep things the way they were with me an' you ...

VALERIE. *(Steps up to Lonnie.)* Well this was fun. Nice to meet ya.

LONNIE. *(Shakes her hand.)* Yeah.

VALERIE. *(Leans into Lonnie.)* Don't hit your son no more. *(Lonnie nods, understandingly. Nickie steps up to Lonnie.)*

NICKIE. Well Lonnie ... no tears ...

LONNIE. No uh ... anger.

NICKIE. No hurt feelings.

LONNIE. Just goodbye.

NICKIE. Good luck. *(They shake hands. Nickie turns to leave with Valerie.)* Oh Jesus Val, did you rememba to turn the sauce down to low before you ...

VALERIE. *(Out the door.)* Yeah yeah afta I heard it bubblin'.

NICKIE. *(Exits behind Valerie.)* Your father will have a ca-niption if it's ruined ...

AL. It's past lunch, Lon-Man, I don't wanna lose my job. Go home. Tell your wife you lo ...

LONNIE. *(Cuts Al off.)* Al, don't tell me what I should tell my wife. I know what I should tell my wife.

AL. *(Smiles.)* Now you know. That's somethin', right? *(Gets closer to Lonnie.)* Am I right? Huh? C'mon, am I right? Look at me ...

LONNIE. *(Looks at Al, smiles.)* Yeah yeah ya sonofabitch, you're right.

AL. Good. Good. *(Al quickly hugs Lonnie, and cries in his arms. Lonnie comforts him. Al pulls away, feeling better. He proceeds to the door then proclaims:)* I feel good. *(Al exits. Lonnie closes the door then turns back into the room very much a man alive.)*

LONNIE. "Now you know. That's something, right?" *(Lights fade as Gospel music is heard coming up. Blackout.)*

END OF PLAY

PROPERTY LIST

Phone answering machine (LONNIE)
Dish towel (LONNIE)
Coins (LONNIE)
Pocketbook (NICKIE)
Baseball bat (NICKIE)
Sunglasses (NICKIE)
Bag of Oreo cookies (VALERIE)
Lunch box (AL)
Photo of Lonnie and Vickie (NICKIE)
Make-up (NICKIE)

ROSEMARY
WITH GINGER

This play is dedicated to
Joel "Riley" Schapira
for clearing the pasture so I
could run with this play.

ROSEMARY WITH GINGER was produced by Moxie Productions (Bonnie Anderson, Laura Manarich, Producers) at Theatre Center East, in Toronto, Canada, in March, 1995. It was directed by Marianne McIsaac; the set design was by William Corcoran and the stage manager was Erica Heyland. The cast was as follows:

ROSEMARY .... Sally Cahill
GINGER .... Laura Manarich

ROSEMARY WITH GINGER was produced by Ensemble Studio Theatre (Curt Dempster, Artistic Director) in New York City, in May, 1994. It was directed by Ron Stetson; the set design was by Michael R. Smith; the costume design was by Lauren Press; the lighting design was by Greg MacPherson; the sound design was by Jeffrey M. Taylor and the stage manager was Judith Sostek. The cast was as follows:

ROSEMARY .... Kristen Griffith
GINGER .... Michaela Murphy

ROSEMARY WITH GINGER was produced by Showtime Networks Inc. in association with The Met Theatre (Risa Bramon Garcia and Jerry Levine, Producers), in Act One, a Festival of 15 New One Act Plays, in Los Angeles, California, in June, 1994. It was directed by Paul McCrane; the set design was by Yael Pardess; the costume design was by Taylor Kincaid Cheek; the lighting design was by Ken Booth; the sound design was by Peter Stenshoel and Charles Dayton and the stage manager was Paul Stein. The cast was as follows:

ROSEMARY ....Susan Barnes
GINGER ....Lucinda Jenney

CHARACTERS

GINGER (woman in her late 30s)
ROSEMARY (sister of Ginger, 40ish)

PLACE

The Peter Pan Diner, Providence, Rhode Island.

TIME

A Friday afternoon in October of 1993.

SETTING

The shell of a diner that prospered in the fifties and sixties and now there's one booth left that is downstage right. The large window (that looks out to Elmwood Avenue) has a huge masking tape X taped to it, bullet holes visible all around the X. Stage left is the counter and among the many things piled atop it include a coffee maker (with coffee) and in the center a small counter-top jukebox. Door to the outside is up right, clump of keys hang from the lock. Up left is the entrance to the rest rooms and kitchen. A pay phone is visible and by the entrance.

Boxes of diner paraphernalia are piled in different areas of the space mixed in with chairs, tables, and counter stools. Menus are strewn about the tiled floor.

All in all, the Peter Pan Diner is down to its last booth, its last waitress, its last song.

"there's no need to watch the
bridges that we're burnin'."

Al Green

ROSEMARY
WITH GINGER

Pre-show lights and music fade. Pause. Lights up on Ginger, up by the entrance, talking into the pay phone.

GINGER. ... 'cause we're closed ... for good ... don't matta since when.... Mrs. Guertin, listen to me ... I can't give you the soup-of-the-day 'cause there is none ... that's right ... so you have to stop callin' an' ... no – no I'm not foolin' you ... I'm here just cleanin' up an' ... *(Sudden knocking at the door. Ginger turns to look.)* Uh listen Mrs. Guertin, you take care a yaself ... I will uh-huh bye ... *(She hangs up and proceeds to the door. She's clad in a skirt, stockings, sneakers, and a plain-looking blouse. She turns the clump of keys and lets in Rosemary.)* Where you been?

ROSEMARY. *(Walks by Ginger.)* You gotta be outta your fuckin' mind still bein' here ...

GINGER. I been callin' an' ...

ROSEMARY. I don't believe I drove my Barretta through this shit neighborhood ...

GINGER. 'Bout time you got in touch with me, don't ya think?

ROSEMARY. Every corna, every fuckin' corna packs-a-guys holdin' their crotches an' eyein' me an' forget stoppin' for stop signs. I had one hand on my gun an' the ...

GINGER. *(Quickly.)* You brought a gun?!

ROSEMARY. Oh please, somebody got you pinned an' pullin' off your jeans there'll be two words comin' outta ya mouth ... "fuckin' shoot him!"

GINGER. You been drinkin', haven't you?

ROSEMARY. This area's been taken over by the Hu-Mong,

41

honey, an' this diner's closed an' you wanna know why?

GINGER. I can smell the blackberry brandy, Rose ...

ROSEMARY. Fuck you an' listen ...

GINGER. I don't wanna listen if you're on one of your drinkin' binges an' ...

ROSEMARY. This diner is closed 'cause the Hu-Mong don't eat meat loaf specials an' don't an' don't have English muffins in their diet an' they hate American chop-suey!

GINGER. Now I know why you didn't get back to me when I ...

ROSEMARY. The Hu-Mong eat people!

GINGER. Oh god, you're in that asshole mood.

ROSEMARY. Yeah well ... *(Rosemary is clad in tight jeans, small white boots, and a jazzed-up jean jacket over a loose-fitting blouse.)* Me an' Raymond the "oran-ga-tan man" got into this big fight an' he's like screamin' in my face not lettin' me talk so he goes like "yeah well you're outta here!" So I busted every mirra in the house ...

GINGER. Look, if you don't wanna do this then ...

ROSEMARY. Get me a coffee, girl, if ya not too busy ...

GINGER. Don't take it out on me 'cause Raymond ...

ROSEMARY. Get me a coffee, Miss, half a cup, black ...

GINGER. *(At the counter.)* Really, if you don't wanna do this with me then ...

ROSEMARY. *(By the booth.)* I'm here! *(Beat.)* I'm here ... *(She slides in the booth while Ginger gets the coffee. Rosemary removes her coat.)*

GINGER. I thought we should do somethin' for ma, yunno, 'cause lately she's been gettin' depressed an' nothin' goes good for her ... then there's you. *(Rosemary picks up a piece of paper from the table and reads.)*

ROSEMARY. "Unsung Mother of the Month Award." *(Ginger walks to the booth with cup of coffee.)*

GINGER. If she wins they'll give her a five-hundred dollar gift certificate to the Shoppers World.

ROSEMARY. You do most of the writin' it, I'm just hidin' from the "oran-ga-tan man" whose gotta be losin' his mind about now with no mirra's an' I flushed his diet pills down the toilet an' just for the hell of it I beat the shit outta his mailbox!

GINGER.   Are you gonna help me?

ROSEMARY.   "Are you gonna help me?" *(She removes a pint of brandy from her pocketbook and adds some to her coffee.)*

GINGER.   So you did drop outta A – A ...

ROSEMARY.   Goddamn people with their sob stories an' – an' everybody wants to hug an' hug an' pray an' pray, it's like my worst nightmare. Rememba when Dad used to say "there's nothin' worse than bein' around reformed drunks" rememba?

GINGER.   You're just like 'im, it's unbelievable.

ROSEMARY.   An that's bad?

GINGER.   Yeah he's dead.

ROSEMARY.   Oh cut it out, will ya?

GINGER.   How soon you forget the horrors you went through an' how you almost died an' how you couldn't stop throwin' up, Jesus Rose!

ROSEMARY.   It's unda control ... *(Drinks.)* An I don't want to talk about it. *(Finishes her drink.)* I'm here at the Peter Pan Diner riskin' my life, my car, my vagina, so let's do this fuckin' thing an' get out.

GINGER.   You got a way a puttin' things that's like so crude.

ROSEMARY.   Speakin' a crude, you an' Harry talkin' yet since the Madonna thing happened?

GINGER.   *(Looks down to paper.)* Let's start this thing ...

ROSEMARY.   *(Smokes.)* You still on the couch?

GINGER.   Rose!

ROSEMARY.   I'm just catchin' up on the news.

GINGER.   YES I'm still on the couch!

ROSEMARY.   I woulda thrown his ass out if it was ...

GINGER.   I got three kids an' no money an' nowheres to go so what am I gonna do?

ROSEMARY.   I'd sleep in a shelter before I'd ...

GINGER.   I put it past me 'cause ... I – I have to, okay?

ROSEMARY.   Good.

GINGER.   I can't leave him right now.

ROSEMARY.   Fine. Don't leave him.

GINGER.   I'm dealin' with it.

ROSEMARY. I got it Ginger, I got it.

GINGER. I don't have to breathe inta the bag no more.

ROSEMARY. Breathin' on your own, good for you.

GINGER. You haven't told anybody, have you?

ROSEMARY. Nobody would believe it so why bother an' fuck it. Look, sorry I brought it up. Let's get started. We grew up here, I don't wanna die here.

GINGER. Yeah ... *(Rosemary looks over the application.)*

ROSEMARY. Play a coupla tunes.

GINGER. There's only one song in the jukebox.

ROSEMARY. It's not Madonna, is it?

GINGER. Fuck you Rose ... *(Rosemary reads the application.)*

ROSEMARY. Says it's due on the ninth.

GINGER. Right.

ROSEMARY. That's like ...

GINGER. Today.

ROSEMARY. *(Looks up.)* So whadda we do? I don't get what we're supposed to do. How do we even start the fuckin' thing?

GINGER. *(Picks up application.)* Says here they want to know about her past, her childhood and "a profile on what she has done for her family to deserve this recognition."

ROSEMARY. Where do you pick up these things?

GINGER. TV. So ... she was born in September ...

ROSEMARY. The tenth.

GINGER. What year?

ROSEMARY. Well she's sixty so sixty from ninety-three ...

GINGER. *(Writes.)* Nineteen thirty-three ...

ROSEMARY. *(Rises.)* In a house.

GINGER. Really?

ROSEMARY. On Federal Hill.

GINGER. In a house?

ROSEMARY. That's what she said.

GINGER. Never knew that.

ROSEMARY. Now you know. *(She is behind the counter looking to make more coffee.)*

GINGER. *(Writing.)* In a house September tenth, nineteen thirty-three, my mother was born in a house on Federal Hill to the parents of ...

44

ROSEMARY. Uh Raffi-ella and ... what was ma's dad's name?

GINGER. Oh uh ... shit, it was ...

ROSEMARY. Died in a gutter ...

GINGER. I know, I know ... I think, John.

ROSEMARY. John what?

GINGER. Ma's maiden name is Walsh ...

ROSEMARY. But she hated that, rememba? So use Nana's maiden name which was Jackavone.

GINGER. *(Writes.)* Born to the parents of John and Raffi-ella Jackavone.

ROSEMARY. Probly not gonna check it anyway.

GINGER. Okay, afta she was born, then what?

ROSEMARY. *(Snaps.)* Ray that fat fuckin' mother-fucka givin' me shit! Cocksucka thinkin' he can push me around anytime somethin' don't go his way, yunno, the prick thinks I'm like Miss yunno Carmella Castration, yunno, like I want these things to happen, mother-fucka! *(Beat.)* THINGS HAVE BEEN VERY ROUGH ON ME LATELY!

GINGER. *(Turns to Rosemary.)* All right, all right ...

ROSEMARY. *(Bangs on the counter.)* Coffee! I need more coffee! Where's the fuckin' help in this place?! *(Ginger rises. Goes to the counter. Rosemary returns to the booth.)* Coffee, half way ... Miss ... *(Ginger is behind the counter getting coffee. Rosemary takes out her cigarettes.)* Can I smoke in here?

GINGER. A course. It's the Peter Pan Diner.

ROSEMARY. *(Dryly.)* The Peter Pan Diner ...

GINGER. I woulda been here twenty years this December.

ROSEMARY. *(Smokes.)* The ladies room. I just rememba the ladies room an' everybody fixin' their underwear 'cause this is where we'd all come afta makin' out in the park.

GINGER. Me an' Harry sat right over there decidin' where we ... uh, wanted to ...

ROSEMARY. Do it? You can say it.

GINGER. You told me not to do it.

ROSEMARY. I told you — it hurts to do it, if you rememba right.

GINGER. An it did.

ROSEMARY. Afta that it hurts in different places. *(Ginger re-*

turns to the booth with more coffee. Sits. Looks back down to the application.)

GINGER.   So uh ... I guess we should go to when she was sickly ...

ROSEMARY.   Yeah sure ...

GINGER.   When she had Saint Vincent's disease ...

ROSEMARY.   What?

GINGER.   Shit, was it Saint Vincent's or Saint Francis?

ROSEMARY.   What was what?

GINGER.   Oh it's a sickness of the nerves but I don't rememba which Saint it is.

ROSEMARY.   Ma had that?

GINGER.   Still has it.

ROSEMARY.   No shit ...

GINGER.   They named it afta a Saint in those days but I can't for the life of rememba uh ...

ROSEMARY.   So this Saint was a nervous bastard?

GINGER.   I don't know but rememba when ma would start to lose it, usually when you pissed her off like the time she found the book on sex under your bed an' she'd ... *(She stands and does Ma.)* "How I got somebody like you, a kid like you, I – I just don't know what I did to deserve thiiiis! Why do you torture me like thiiiiiis?!" *(She trembles a bit then looks at Rosemary.)*

ROSEMARY.   *(Beat, then.)* That stinks Gin' ... was more like ... *(She stands and does Ma.)* "You're a pig! You're no good! You come from Hell! You're the curse my mother put on me!"

GINGER.   Oh right right I forgot about the curse thing ...

ROSEMARY.   Fuckin' spit be comin' outta her mouth, eyes bulgin' like a fuckin' frog an' you're tellin' me that, that some Saint acted that way?

GINGER.   I don't know 'bout the Saint havin' it but don't matta ... okay, where are we? Um ...

ROSEMARY.   *(Sits.)* What a life ...

GINGER.   *(Writing.)* So she was sickly an' very skinny from bein' sickly an' afta that ... uh ... her father was found dead drunk or – or just dead in a gutta on the corna of ...

ROSEMARY.   Down the street. Corna of Peace and Broad.

GINGER. Froze to death.

ROSEMARY. They found him with no shoes on.

GINGER. So I should say someone stole his shoes?

ROSEMARY. Someone did.

GINGER. So I should write it?

ROSEMARY. Write it for Chrissakes!

GINGER. I don't know, Jesus!

ROSEMARY. "So I should write it? I should write it?"

GINGER. I was askin' a simple ...

ROSEMARY. You been on the couch too long, girl.

GINGER. Okay okay an' ma was how old then?

ROSEMARY. He gets the bed and you get the couch?

GINGER. I think she was around eight. I'll write eight.

ROSEMARY. Eight's when everythin' starts to go bad so say eight.

GINGER. I wrote it.

ROSEMARY. I know.

GINGER. So at eight ...

ROSEMARY. Eight.

GINGER. She went through this.

ROSEMARY. Dead father.

GINGER. No father at eight.

ROSEMARY. He was an asshole.

GINGER. I don't put that down.

ROSEMARY. No shit.

GINGER. Just ... he died when she was eight.

ROSEMARY. Froze to death.

GINGER. I did put that in.

ROSEMARY. Ma said he was an asshole.

GINGER. I never heard ma say asshole.

ROSEMARY. Actually she said "prick."

GINGER. Ma said "prick?"

ROSEMARY. "Ma said prick?"

GINGER. *(Rises from booth.)* I hate it when you drink, I really do. You get that look in your eyes that's nothin' but trouble.

ROSEMARY. I don't know why we're doin' this – this thing 'cause it's not gonna affect the way ma deals with me anyways

SO ...

GINGER. So you think by raggin' on me is gonna ... what? Me an' Harry got a problem an' I made the big mistake a tellin' you an' then you think you can throw it up in my face anytime you want with – with that fuckin' smirk that goes with it!

ROSEMARY. I can't help it, okay, every time I see the piture a you comin' in your house an' seein' him with his pants down an'– an' ...

GINGER. I don't feel like relivin' this right now!

ROSEMARY. (Rises.) When you look at him, his hands, his face, his eyes, don't you get fuckin' repulsed?

GINGER. We got a problem ...

ROSEMARY. Uh-huh, fine ...

GINGER. We're gonna deal with it when ... when we can an' which is more than you're doin' ...

ROSEMARY. (Looking out window.) I deal.

GINGER. (Wiping counter.) Yeah yeah right yeah you deal ...

ROSEMARY. I do. I don't let nothin' slide.

GINGER. Yeah dealin' for you is bustin' mirra's in your boyfriends house an' an' back to drinkin' afta almost dyin' an' fightin' with your first husband an' his new wife over the kids you ... (She stops. Pause. Rosemary turns to her.)

ROSEMARY. That I ... what?

GINGER. That you yunno just ... just not bein' stable somewhere, I don't know ...

ROSEMARY. I love my kids. You sayin' I don't love my kids?

GINGER. I would never say that, god ...

ROSEMARY. Never?

GINGER. No!

ROSEMARY. 'Cause I love my kids 'cause they're my kids! (Pause. Ginger returns to the booth. Looks down at the application.)

GINGER. (Finally.) Ma was eight when her father died. Where do we go from there? (Beat.) When she met Dad? An' she was sixteen, right?

ROSEMARY. (Looking out window.) Yup.

GINGER. Okay um an' he was ...

ROSEMARY. Probly eighteen.

48

GINGER. *(Writing.)* Eighteen.

ROSEMARY. Ma's mother wanted to kill him.

GINGER. So she's sixteen an' livin' alone with her mother an' meets Joe Quinn, gets pregnant an' then what? They married then ...

ROSEMARY. Ran away to Boston.

GINGER. Really?

ROSEMARY. Really. Ran away. Lived there. Had me. Came back. With me. Moved to Althea Street. He drove a cab. She was makin' potato chips for the A&P ...

GINGER. Should I put in 'bout ma goin' through some tough times yunno an' havin' all those mis-carriages afta havin' me an' you by the time she was uh twenty-three, twenty-four ...

ROSEMARY. You gonna put stuff in 'bout dad smackin' the shit out of her whenever things didn't go his way?

GINGER. *(Beat.)* Oh. Should I put that um ... she was abused?

ROSEMARY. *(Walks to the booth.)* Oh married an' pregnant at sixteen, worked at the A&P, had two kids an' a bunch of mis-carriages and was an' abused woman! Hey! Give that lady a closet full-a-clothes! She is truly amazing! *(Silence. She walks over to the counter then sits facing Ginger.)*

GINGER. You wanna keep going?

ROSEMARY. I ask that to myself every day.

GINGER. You know what I'm talkin' about.

ROSEMARY. Do you know what I'm talkin' about?

GINGER. You know what I'm talkin' about.

ROSEMARY. Do you know what I'm talkin' about?

GINGER. Jesus! Are you on those stupid pills again?!

ROSEMARY. No I'm off. One day I just couldn't stop playin' with myself so I stopped takin' 'em.

GINGER. The things you say ...

ROSEMARY. It's the truth. I always tell the truth. *(Beat.)* How 'bout you? You always tell the truth?

GINGER. You got that look on your face again. That Dad look.

ROSEMARY. You tell the truth, don't you?

GINGER. You wanna keep doin' this or not?

ROSEMARY. I'm here, aren't I?

GINGER. I – I really thought for a minute yunno that it'd be kinda nice ... me an' you in our old neighborhood an' – an' away from kids an' men an' just ... just together alone for a change in this place where we'd done stuff ... me askin' you my big sista for advice on guys an' ...

ROSEMARY. Told ya not to marry Harry, didn't I?

GINGER. *(Beat.)* Maybe you did. *(Beat.)* I thought that I'd put in how ma was ... well how everybody came to her with their problems, that our house was an open house.

ROSEMARY. Our house was a dirty house.

GINGER. No, you know what I mean, right?

ROSEMARY. Our house wasn't even a house, it was an apartment.

GINGER. Oh right – right.

ROSEMARY. Other people had houses.

GINGER. That's good ... *(Writes.)* Always ... lived ... in ... an ... apartment ...

ROSEMARY. Could hear everythin' an' everybody up an' down an' all around. Would go to sleep to "Leo, now Leo!" And Leo would yell "wait Flo, I gotta find it first!"

GINGER. An Mrs. Auerbach downstairs with the polio ... *(Beat.)* Oh that's great! Ma helped her walk!

ROSEMARY. You gonna put in how ma was on my back day in an' day out an' how she tortured me an' ...

GINGER. I can't put that in here, she'd lose.

ROSEMARY. Fuck it. I can't get into this. I'm gettin' hungry. Menu please, Miss ...

GINGER. *(Writing.)* There's nothin' to eat.

ROSEMARY. I want a turkey club with tomatoes an' mayo on the side, French fries well done and the bacon too but not black an' spare my sandwich from the toothpicks, I hate the fuckin' toothpicks an' oh yeah to drink I'll have a coffee cabinet an' don't forget to bring the vinegar for the fries!

GINGER. Only have crackers.

ROSEMARY. Well that sucks! *(Stands suddenly.)* One time! One time I pulled Laurie's hair and it was only 'cause I was grabbin' for her arm an' she like moved an' I got her hair instead yunno, it was a mistake. I wouldn't pull her hair, an' – an' ...

GINGER.   Okay, okay ...

ROSEMARY.   An that bitch of a bitch wife a Brads — Betsy that cow, makin' it like I messed up when Little Brad cracked open his head 'cause I didn't make sure he was wearin' a bike helmet! I mean since when did this become a law, this bike helmet thing?!

GINGER.   I ...

ROSEMARY.   *(Quickly.)* They're my kids! Not Betsy's, they're mine!

GINGER.   I know, I know ...

ROSEMARY.   *(Goes to booth.)* Wait, just wait till she hears that me an' Brad screwed only like about two months ago! They wanna fuck with me then I'll fuck right back!

GINGER.   You're kiddin' me ...

ROSEMARY.   I bumped inta him at Memories this one night the Five Satins were playin' an' wham out in the parkin' lot an' in his truck we didn't stop for an hour!

GINGER.   Oh.

ROSEMARY.   *(Drinks.)* An it was great too an' he was sayin' all kinda shit 'bout how he still loves me an' misses me an' wishes there was a way, yunno, you shoulda heard 'im, right?

GINGER.   You did it in the parkin' lot of Memories with Ray in the Club?

ROSEMARY.   The "oran-ga-tan man" was too busy kissin' up to the Five Satins an' tryin' to jew-em-outta their askin' price.... He didn't even know I was gone, the fat fuck!

GINGER.   God ...

ROSEMARY.   *(Beat.)* Fuck you "god" fuck you.

GINGER.   Wait a ...

ROSEMARY.   Like I'm some pervert for doin' it, fuck you too. Your husband's got his lips to the – the TV an' his cock in hand an' there's somethin' wrong with me?!

GINGER.   I didn't say there was ...

ROSEMARY.   *(Moves from booth.)* Tend to your own garden 'fore you start comin' down on what I do!

GINGER.   I wasn't comin' down on ...

ROSEMARY.   Least I was dealin' with flesh!

GINGER.   Oh god what are you...?!

ROSEMARY.   The time was right an' an' maybe the moon was right an' it's not like I ... yunno, didn't do it with him before. It was familiar an' it was real ...

GINGER.   *(Stands.)* You done attackin' me?

ROSEMARY.   I'm not attackin' you. I didn't like your tone, that's all.

GINGER.   I mean I got enough bullshit in my life an' one day I daydreamed me an' you with ma at The Shoppers World pickin' out clothes for her an' – an' earrings an' ... but you got a way a turnin' it all around 'cause you don't give a shit 'bout nothin' but ... then seein' you back to drinkin' is depressin' enough ...

ROSEMARY.   Yeah. Like you talkin' to Brad.

GINGER.   What?

ROSEMARY.   Like you talkin' to Brad.

GINGER.   What are...?

ROSEMARY.   Like you an' Brad havin' a little talk about Rosemary. *(She pulls out a letter from her pocket.)*

GINGER.   I ... we ...

ROSEMARY.   I woke up this smornin' to a Sheriff servin' me with an affadavit from Brad ... *(Reads from the affadavit.)* "... an' my ex-sista in-law Ginger Willis is in agreement with my decision to pursue custody of the children. In our phone conversations she agrees with me that the children's safety and well-being is in danger if my ex-wife is drinking."

GINGER.   Oh god ...

ROSEMARY.   *(Continuing.)* "My ex-sista in-law spoke at length of Rosemary's past drinkin' problems stating to me that her sister's mental condition has gotten worse since being with Raymond Perretti, her live-in boyfriend who owns the night-club Memories an' likes to drink an' party ..." *(She pauses then crosses to the booth.)* I'm gonna scratch out Raymond Perretti an' put "since being with the oran-ga-tan man ..."

GINGER.   *(Takes a step to Rosemary.)* Rose, he's really worried an' – an' ...

ROSEMARY.   Fuck you.

GINGER. He called an' I ...

ROSEMARY. I'm outta here. *(She is putting stuff back in her pocketbook. Ginger gets closer to her.)*

GINGER. Listen to me Rose ... Rosemary, look at me! *(Rosemary looks at her.)* I .... Brad called me an' we talked or he did most a the talkin' an' I don't know what you got in your head about it but it was ... he talked about a temporary custody thing an' wondrin' when you're gonna get help. I – I think he is really worried, uh I don't think he's tryin' to be mean or ... anyway ... um ... *(She sits. Stares down at the application. Pause.)*

ROSEMARY. *(Softly.)* I ... I ... keep hearin' ... my my kid's voices ...

GINGER. I know ...

ROSEMARY. "Mommy, where are we goin'?" "Mommy, why are you drivin' so fast?" "Mommy please don't drive so fast."

GINGER. Rose ...

ROSEMARY. "Just be quiet an' – an' Laurie make sure your seat belt is on tight ..."

GINGER. What are you...?

ROSEMARY. "Mommy, it's scary, you're scarin' me ..." "Mommy, why'd you take us outta school?" "Mommy please, we want daddy ..."

GINGER. This happened?

ROSEMARY. "We're goin' to Rocky Point Cliffs, kids. Daddy says I never do anythin' with you kids so we're goin' to Rocky Point Cliffs an' look out over the ocean, okay?"

GINGER. *(Nervously.)* When did this happen?

ROSEMARY. "Even Auntie Ginger says I'm not a good mother."

GINGER. *(Stands.)* When did this happen?!

ROSEMARY. "But Mommy, we go to school today, we got masks to make for Halloween an' ... mommy bring us back!"

GINGER. Are they in the car?! *(She runs to the window and looks out.)*

ROSEMARY. "You sit down Laurie! I am your mother so you listen to me, now sit before I...."

GINGER. Stop it Rose!

ROSEMARY. "I am your mother.... I am your mother...."

GINGER. You stop it god damn it!

ROSEMARY. "It's too windy up here mommy, the water is so ... is so gray ..." *(Ginger grabs a coin from the counter then runs to the pay phone.)* "I'm your mother, kids ... don't be afraid of me, no need to be afraid of me ..." *(Ginger is dialing.)* "Just look out, okay, not down ... look straight out."

GINGER. *(On phone.)* C'mon, pick up, pick up ...

ROSEMARY. "Okay, now hold hands kids ... an' – an' I'm gonna step over here ..."

GINGER. *(Into phone.)* Hello! Brad!

ROSEMARY. "... 'cause I wanna take your piture ..."

GINGER. *(Into phone.)* Listen, where are the kids?!

ROSEMARY. "Laurie, step back, Hon ... you're still too close to Mommy ..."

GINGER. Call the school then call me back at the diner! *(Hangs up phone.)*

ROSEMARY. "... now c'mon, back up for your mother, I want the best piture I can get to show people my kids."

GINGER. You cut it out Rose!

ROSEMARY. "Nice one, now I want ya to turn around so I get a piture a you both lookin' out over the ocean ..."

GINGER. *(By the phone.)* I never said those things!

ROSEMARY. "I'm gettin' closer, okay, but don't turn around an' look at me ..."

GINGER. He just put that stuff in there!

ROSEMARY. "Laurie, don't look at Mommy I said!" *(Ginger turns to face the phone.)*

GINGER. Please god no don't let this happen oh God, Oh God I ...

ROSEMARY. "I'm right behind you now don't move an' don't look back an' ..." *(Phone rings. Ginger gets it.)*

GINGER. Yeah!

ROSEMARY. "Here we go, ready?"

GINGER. *(Listens, calmer.)* Okay ... yeah ... nothin' I ... *(Ginger turns to look at Rosemary. Rosemary picks up her coffee and drinks.)*

ROSEMARY. Ah, that hit the spot ...

GINGER. *(On the phone.)* Sure ... okay, bye ... *(Hangs up the phone.)*

ROSEMARY. Well, fuck you Ginger.

GINGER. Doin' that ... makes you feel, what? Happy?

ROSEMARY. I'll be happy as soon as that turkey club gets here.

GINGER. I don't believe what you just did!

ROSEMARY. You're helpin' 'im take my kids from me!

GINGER. No!

ROSEMARY. You turned against me!

GINGER. *(Suddenly.)* WHO was at your house when you couldn't stop throwin' up an' WHO called the rescue squad an' WHO cleaned up the blood you was spittin' up?! *(She moves closer to Rosemary.)* It was me who stopped you from jumpin' out the winda an' it was me who sat on you screamin' for the nurse while you spit in my face an' afta three days a that I stood back an' saw you gettin' all the flowers an' everybody loves Rosemary an' Rosemary says, "Ginger put these over there" an' "Ginger watch for the nurses while I sneak a smoke" and I did it but deep down I was there waiting for a hey-by-the-way-thanks-for-what-you-did-for-me but Rosemary was too busy flirtin' with the doctors to notice her only sista who as usual took time from her own family to be with Rosemary 'cause Rosemary needed me ... *(Rosemary prepares to leave.)* "No Harry I can't, I gotta help Rosemary move." "I'll be right back, I gotta pick up Rose's kids." "Harry, nobody can find Rosemary so I gotta go ..." *(Rosemary straightens up.)* Then that day that stupid thing with Harry happened ....

ROSEMARY. Open the fuckin' door Ginger ...

GINGER. I ... I walk into my house and ...

ROSEMARY. An' Harry's pants are down an' he's up to the Madonna video beatin' off to the beat, guys do that shit ...

GINGER. I DON'T LIKE IT OKAY!

ROSEMARY. I really have to go so if you'd ...

GINGER. Like I'm a fuckin' tard for bein' old-fashioned an' what is everythin' comin' to?! Why is everybody goin' fuckin' mental?! *(Rosemary starts for the door but Ginger gets there first and takes out the keys from the lock.)*

55

ROSEMARY. *(Turns back to the booth.)* Oh great. Held hostage in the Peter Pan Diner.

GINGER. So me an' Harry ... we're standin' there ... like two people separated by a winda ...

ROSEMARY. Oh shit ...

GINGER. An lookin' at him I got right there ... I don't love this guy an' probly never really did .... An' I been doin' house-shit for seventeen years, seventeen years a – a him drivin' his oil truck an' me shovin' food in front a people an' as a wife I had nothin' ... an' it galled me knowin' you told me not to marry him, it galled me an' I ...

ROSEMARY. Whaddaya want me to say about all this?!

GINGER. If I leave him where do I go? An' – an' what about the kids an' – an' ma ... shit, I – I go out there an' what? Look for a guy an' say "save me please an' oh by the way I got three kids an' I been havin' anxiety attacks an' oh yeah oh yeah ... I – I ... I was told that I got uh two lumps ... in my right breast ... *(Rosemary looks to Ginger, concernedly. Ginger looks at her.)* That's where I was before I ... I was at the uh Doctor Ferrante an' ... I even joked with him 'cause his hands felt so warm on my ... an' I said somethin' like um ... "Jesus, maybe I shoulda picked up a bottle of wine 'fore I came, right?" An uh he didn't seem to hear me ... he just kept pressin' this one spot an' I could see in his eyes that uh-oh, what's a matta? An he told me ... not one lump ... but two an' I cried right there and he was nice enough to um hold me for a minute an' I ... all I was thinkin' was about my kids an' wantin' to be in my house with my family an' I somehow managed to drive an' I walk in feelin' uh light-headed an' I catch Harry an' uh ... *(Rosemary is visibly upset. Ginger steps closer to her.)* And Rosemary ... fuck ... you ... too. *(With that Ginger sits. Wipes her eyes with a napkin. Rosemary stares at her. Silence.)*

ROSEMARY. *(Finally.)* All a lie?

GINGER. My life with Harry stinks an' the Madonna thing happened.

ROSEMARY. No lumps?

GINGER. Just wanted to see if you gave a shit is all.

ROSEMARY. *(Beat.)* That was good.

GINGER. Good teacher, don't ya think?

ROSEMARY. Guess.

GINGER. Rose, I'm just gonna say it. You're a real real shitty mother an' you're a drunk that's made you into a maniac but you know what? I'm gonna tell you somethin' right here an' it probly goes back to when we was kids when you would hum a song close to my ear when mom and dad were fighting so I wouldn't hear 'em ... an' I – I love you as much as I love my kids. I'd give you my last breath an' ... *(Sits back.)* Sorry for gettin' sappy here an' I would never turn against you. Never. I said things to Brad that well I shoulda been sayin' to you but I chickened out 'cause in your way you can make people afraid to say what should be said. Like dad was ... *(Beat.)* I won't hug you or nothin' 'cause I know you hate that ... *(Beat.)* You all right?

ROSEMARY. Yeah – yeah ... *(Beat.)* I'm just ... yunno, I'm afraid ...

GINGER. Makes two of us ... but hey ma went through some tough times, right? *(Rosemary nods. Beat.)* I gotta pee. *(She rises and proceeds to the rest room. On her way she stops at the counter and bangs the side of the jukebox then exits into the bathroom. A couple of beats of silence then Al Green's song, "For the Good Times"* fills the diner. Rosemary is crying. Walks around to gather herself. Pause. Ginger exits the bathroom.)*

ROSEMARY. My turkey club ready yet?

GINGER. Sorry Miss ... the kitchen is closed. *(Ginger sits in the booth.)*

ROSEMARY. *(Approaches Ginger.)* Let's do the thing for ma someplace else.

GINGER. Where?

ROSEMARY. Memories? *(Ginger can't believe it.)* I'm kiddin', I'm kiddin'. *(Rosemary laughs. Sits.)* Brad's probly gonna get custody, huh?

GINGER. Yeah Rose, probly. But it's a temporary thing.

ROSEMARY. Yeah. *(Beat.)* I'll bounce back.

---

* See Special Note on Songs and Recordings on copyright page.

GINGER.   You always do. *(Beat. Rosemary extends her hand out to her sister.)*

ROSEMARY.   Hang on Ginger ... *(Ginger grabs hold of her sister's hand.)*

GINGER.   I'm hangin' on Rosemary ... *(Lights fade to black as the song increases in volume.)*

END OF PLAY

PROPERTY LIST

Clumps of keys on chain (GINGER)
Cup of coffee (GINGER)
Application paper (ROSEMARY)
Pocketbook with pint of brandy (ROSEMARY)
Coffee maker and coffee (GINGER)
Cigarettes (ROSEMARY)
Matches or lighter (ROSEMARY)
Cloth (GINGER)
Coin (GINGER)
Napkin (GINGER)

FACE
DIVIDED

This play is dedicated to the children born to seventeen-year-old mothers.

FACE DIVIDED was produced by Ensemble Studio Theatre (Curt Dempster, Artistic Director) as part of their Marathon 1991, in New York City, in May, 1991. It was directed by Risa Bramon Garcia; the set design was by David K. Gallo; the costume design was by David E. Sawaryn; the lighting design was by Greg MacPherson; the sound design was by One Dream and the stage manager was Elisa Ann Konstatin. The cast was as follows:

NURSE SUE WILCOX .... Trazana Beverley
DEBBIE IRONS .... Kellie Overbey
FREDDIE IRONS .... Sam Rockwell

CHARACTERS

Debbie Irons (20)
Sue Wilcox (African-American; late 30s)
Freddie Irons (21)
Voice of Hospital Receptionist (female)

PLACE

Saint Joseph's Hospital, Providence, Rhode Island
Just after midnight
Summer of 1989

SETTING

Small examination room in the emergency ward. Walls are white. Fluorescent lights over an examining table that's center stage. Upstage left is a sink with a medicine cabinet above it. Upstage center is the door to the outside corridor. A simple chair is downstage right. A garbage can is downstage left. A wall phone is upstage right.

FACE DIVIDED

Scene: In the blackness someone is heard trying to find a good song on their radio.

Pause. Then fluorescent lights flicker on and up bright on Debbie Irons, who's atop the examining table with her radio/ tape player in her lap.

INTERCOM. Mrs. Campbell, dial 8-3-1, Mrs. Campbell, dial 8-3-1. *(Debbie looks up, disgustedly. She hates the voice. She sits up, and jumps from the table. Lights a cigarette, and paces about the space. She is clad in tight jeans and a tight-fitting top. Debbie takes a moment to examine her face in the mirror above the sink then stubs out the cigarette. She moves to the door and swings it open — sounds of a rush in the room. Debbie looks both ways then yell.)*

DEBBIE. I'M STILL HERE IN CASE ANYBODY FORGOT! *(Beat.)* DEBBIE IRONS! HEY! NURSE!

NURSE'S VOICE. Stop that yelling!

DEBBIE. But can you tell me about my daughter and ... *(Door opens all the way revealing Nurse Sue Wilcox, an African-American woman in her late 30s. She is holding a clipboard and moves Debbie back into the room. Door closes.)*

SUE. Don't go yellin' out there like that. What's the matter with you yelling out there like that?!

DEBBIE. I been in here since ...

SUE. You think this is a high school corridor?

DEBBIE. I know what it is.

SUE. Then act like you do.

DEBBIE. Is Jess all right. *(Sue is washing her hands.)*

SUE. Uh-huh.

DEBBIE. You ain't heard nothin' from my husband yet?

65

SUE.   No.

DEBBIE.   Fuck! I wish he'd hurry up an' get here!

SUE.   Relax. He'll be ...

DEBBIE.   I called the club three times!

SUE.   Okay, okay, listen, we've got to go over the info you wrote down for me earlier because your handwriting is worse than some doctors around here so ...

DEBBIE.   Jess is all right?

SUE.   Yes. Now we've got to get ...

DEBBIE.   That fuckin' Freddie, I'm gonna kill that sonofabitch, always doin' what he wants to do! An' the jerk isn't around when something like this happens, what happened tonight.

SUE.   Stop working yourself up. I need you to help me for a minute or two so please have a seat. *(Debbie stands still. Glares at Sue. Sue looks down at clipboard.)* No medical coverage?

DEBBIE.   Nope.

SUE.   You on Welfare?

DEBBIE.   Just food stamps.

SUE.   So you're on Welfare.

DEBBIE.   We just get food stamps.

SUE.   Uh ... you live on ... *(Looks closer at the clipboard.)*

DEBBIE.   Eighteen Olney Street, first floor behind the closed-down brewery. *(Beat.)* If he don't get here real soon I'm ...

SUE.   I can't read this. What does your husband do for work?

DEBBIE.   He's a bass player in a band three nights a week an' he janitors durin' the day.

SUE.   So no medical benefits from his ...

DEBBIE.   It's unda the table stuff for now 'til he gets his diploma from night school. Least that's what he says.

SUE.   My brother in-law is a drummer in a band.

DEBBIE.   He's got all the answers while I got the walls and pampers!

SUE.   The Pep-Tones. You ever hear of them?

DEBBIE.   *(Beat.)* The what?

SUE.   Pep-Tones. *(Awkward beat between them.)*

DEBBIE.   Pep-Tones.

SUE.   They do fifties kind of ... and uh ... some Flamingos.

Platters. Temptations. *(Beat. Sue looks down.)* Okay, let's see ...
(Reads from clipboard.) Father deceased, mother lives in Washington Park, okay, okay, you were born in blah-blah blah, that's all right. You don't work, you didn't finish high school, your phone number is 9-4-3-2-1-4 ... uh ...

DEBBIE.   Five! 9-4-3-2-1-4-5!

SUE.   *(Continues.)* Jess was born here in August, she's three years old, okay, okay ... *(Looks up.)* Any complications during your pregnancy?

DEBBIE.   I hated it. It was real hot that summa.

SUE.   Any complications during the pregnancy?

DEBBIE.   *(Dryly.)* Nope.

SUE.   Any complications during the delivery?

DEBBIE.   Who knows, yunno, they knocked me out, they waked me up an' handed me a baby. *(Sue looks at Debbie for a beat.)*

SUE.   Uh-huh.

DEBBIE.   You got kids?

SUE.   Two girls.

DEBBIE.   My stupid sista, right? "An' – an' Russ was there watchin' an helpin' me breathe an' when Heather came out, me an' Russ just cried at this miracle we made as one!" She says ,"Oh Debbie, you just gotta do it the way a dog does it."

SUE.   She was probably referring to the panting-breathing exercise that ...

DEBBIE.   I says, "that mean you licked it clean afta it came out?" My mother almost shit.

SUE.   You said that in front of your mother?

DEBBIE.   We don't get along so it don't matta.

INTERCOM.   Mrs. Campbell, dial 8-3-1, Mrs. Campbell, dial 8-3-1.

SUE.   Let's go over what you told me earlier.

DEBBIE.   About what happened?

SUE.   You said it was ten o'clock.

DEBBIE.   Little afta. Aleven, right? Wait, what time is it now. It's aleven ... is that what I said before? Ten?

SUE.   Uh-huh.

DEBBIE.   What time is it now?

SUE. Twelve thirty-five.

DEBBIE. Shit! An' he isn't here yet?! I bet that stupid tard of a bartenda didn't give him ...

SUE. Sit down Debbie! Now we need your cooperation starting this minute! Do you understand me?! *(A glaring beat between them. Sue reads from the clipboard.)* "I heard Jess get out of bed."

DEBBIE. Right. She was goin' to the bathroom.

SUE. She say anything to you?

DEBBIE. Nope.

SUE. Then what?

DEBBIE. She ... well I heard this ... I heard a noise an' -- an' that was her fallin' down the cellar stairs.

SUE. So she opened ...

DEBBIE and SUE. The wrong door.

DEBBIE. An' I'll give ya one guess who left the cellar door unlocked!

SUE. The bathroom door being right next to the ...

DEBBIE. Right next to the cellar door.

SUE. No lights on?

DEBBIE. None. All dark.

SUE. So after you heard the noise you ...

DEBBIE. I ran an' turned on the light in the hallway and seen the cellar door open an' ...

SUE. Did you yell to a neighbor for help or ...

DEBBIE. Can tell you never been down Olney Street.

SUE. All right, so you called the Rescue.

DEBBIE. Right, right, but before that I put her head in the sink unda the runnin' water an' she opened her eyes.

SUE. That was quick thinkin'.

DEBBIE. Yeah well my mother used to do it to me 'cause I used to pass out when I would cry an' stuff.

SUE. So you did that then called the Rescue.

DEBBIE. Yup.

SUE. *(Reads from clipboard.)* "Then I ... I picked up my ..." What? Raincoat? What is this word?

DEBBIE. *(Looks at clipboard.)* Radio. I picked up my radio.

SUE. Radio. Okay. I see that.

DEBBIE. I knew it was warm.

SUE.   The radio was warm?

DEBBIE.   Warm out. Warm out. I didn't need my jacket 'cause I knew it was warm out.

SUE.   So you picked up the radio.

DEBBIE.   Do you get that?!

SUE.   Don't get snotty with me girl.

DEBBIE.   I'm pissed, all right?

SUE.   I understand that but ... *(Phone buzzes. Sue gets up.)* It's been a crazy night around here. *(She picks up the phone.)* Yes ...

DEBBIE.   He betta fuckin' get here.

SUE.   He will. *(Into phone.)* Uh-huh, uh-huh ...

DEBBIE.   I'm tired a doin' everythin' alone.

SUE.   *(On phone.)* Okay, I see, uh-huh ... *(She hangs up.)* Listen to me now ... *(Beat.)* Jess is resting upstairs in Pediatrics and a call has been made to a Doctor Burton who is a Neurologist.

DEBBIE.   Yup, yup.

SUE.   When your husband gets here, he has to fill out some info for me then we go upstairs.

DEBBIE.   How come I can't go up there now?

SUE.   We're waiting for your husband so we can take care of all this.

INTERCOM.   Doctor Guerra, pick up line six. Doctor Guerra, line six.

DEBBIE.   Can ya shut her up?! I can't stand her voice!

SUE.   *(At the door.)* Can I get you a soda or something?

DEBBIE.   Doughnuts.

SUE.   Cafeteria's closed.

DEBBIE.   Anythin' like candy bars or chips, shit like that?

SUE.   Ginger ale, juice or coffee.

DEBBIE.   No coke?

SUE.   I would've said it.

DEBBIE.   Ginger ale. *(Beat.)* You don't like me, do you?

SUE.   I'd go crazy if I went around judging the characters who come in and out of here.

DEBBIE.   Yeah but admit it, you don't like me, I can tell those things.

SUE. Honey I'm a Nurse and ... *(Suddenly the door opens and enter Freddie Irons in ripped jeans and a jean jacket over a rock and roll tee-shirt. Noise of the corridor fills the room.)*

FREDDIE. All right! I'm here!

DEBBIE. About fuckin' time you got here! *(Sue prevents Debbie from getting at Freddie.)*

FREDDIE. What's been going on?!

DEBBIE. Fuckin' jerk! I been here alone! *(Debbie makes an attempt to slap at Freddie.)*

SUE. That's enough!

FREDDIE. Relax!

DEBBIE. Asshole!

FREDDIE. She said that's enough! *(Sue moves Debbie away from Freddie.)*

SUE. Now you don't go upstairs until you've calmed down. Is that clear? *(Debbie hears her. Backs off. Beat. Sue turns to Freddie. Hands him the clipboard.)* Fill this page out for me and I'll be back. *(Sue exits. Silence for a beat.)*

DEBBIE. Where you been?!

FREDDIE. I'm here!

DEBBIE. Where you been?!

FREDDIE. Whaddaya talkin' about?! I'm here!

DEBBIE. I been doin' this on my own!

FREDDIE. I want to know about Jess! You tell me!

DEBBIE. They're lookin' at her upstairs an' told me she's restin' an' they're waitin' for another kinda doctor to come. She fell down the cellar stairs 'cause the door was unlocked! The fuckin' door was unlocked!

FREDDIE. *(Tiredly.)* Ah shit ...

DEBBIE. Yeah "ah shit" is right!

FREDDIE. I mean what the fuck happened Debbie?! You weren't watchin' her?!

DEBBIE. It wasn't me who left the door unlocked!

FREDDIE. I always lock that door! Always!

DEBBIE. Tanight you forgot.

FREDDIE. Can't believe this.

DEBBIE. She got up to go to the bathroom an' just grabbed the cellar door thinkin' it was the bathroom door an' went down.

FREDDIE.   Shit! Fuck! Fuck!

DEBBIE.   I was in bed an' heard her fallin'. I got real scared 'cause at first I thought the Spic from upstairs was tryin' ta break in an' I jumped outta bed with the bat an' saw Jess's bed empty an' the cellar door open. I ran down an' in my mind I'm thinkin' "why isn't Freddie here?! Freddie should be here!"

FREDDIE.   So what've they been tellin' you?

DEBBIE.   This nurse says Jess is restin' an' they been keepin' me in here like I'm a fuckin' nobody sayin' they was waitin' for you. *(Freddie paces the room a bit. Tears off his jacket, then pauses to look at the radio.)*

FREDDIE.   You brought the radio?

DEBBIE.   So what?

FREDDIE.   Wha'd you bring the radio for?

DEBBIE.   I thought someone might steal it an' it's the best thing I got! Anythin' else?

FREDDIE.   I'm just wondrin', all right? I almost got killed drivin' here! Lookit my hands, they're fuckin' shakin'!

DEBBIE.   You do that roach in the ashtray?

FREDDIE.   An' I got this cold in my stomach, like a shiver.

DEBBIE.   Did you smoke the half a joint in the ashtray?

FREDDIE.   You're talkin' about gettin' stoned right now?

DEBBIE.   We're gonna need a buzz when we get outta here is all I'm ...

FREDDIE.   *(Cuts her off.)* I don't wanna talk about that shit right now! So keep quiet for a minute if ya can! *(He is looking at the clipboard. Debbie stares at him. Pause.)*

DEBBIE.   I can smell the club on ya from over here.

FREDDIE.   Good.

DEBBIE.   "Good."

FREDDIE.   I always lock that door.

DEBBIE.   Yeah well ...

FREDDIE.   I lock it 'cause a Jess an' for no other reason.

DEBBIE.   I wasn't down there.

FREDDIE.   I came up afta practicin' an' rememba hearin' you on the phone with Kathy Martin yakkin' about some shit

71

an' ...

DEBBIE. We weren't yakkin' about shit!

FREDDIE. It's always shit with you an' her!

DEBBIE. I was askin' her about a dentist I could see 'cause my tooth has been leakin' out gas again!

FREDDIE. Look in the phone book!

DEBBIE. Oh I can't ask my best friend about ...

FREDDIE. She's a do-nothin' an' a troublemaker!

DEBBIE. You sure didn't think that when she gave us her cellar for our weddin' ceremony!

FREDDIE. Forget this. I don't know why I'm bringin' her up. I'm nervous ...

DEBBIE. Kathy Martin has done a lot for us.

FREDDIE. Yeah, yeah ... *(Freddie goes to the door. Opens it. Noise enters. He looks both ways down the corridor.)* Fuckin' zoo ... *(He lets the door fall shut. He turns to Debbie and stares at her for a long beat.)*

DEBBIE. *(Little nervous.)* What? *(Beat.)* Freddie? *(Beat.)* What?

FREDDIE. *(Softly.)* Tooth still hurt?

DEBBIE. *(Softly.)* Kinda. *(Freddie goes to her at the examining table.)*

FREDDIE. Open up. *(She does. He looks in her mouth. Pause.)* Leakin' gas. Never know what ta look for when I do this. *(Debbie pulls him to her and hugs him, desperately. They remain like this for a few beats.)* You gotta stop eatin' all that junk, yunno. Some people in the papers an' shit say it makes ya do stupid things an' ... *(She pushes him away from her.)*

DEBBIE. I'm so sick a you puttin' me down, puttin' me down. I been trew a lot tonight with ridin' in the Rescue with Jess an' all the questions an' callin YOU an' tryin to get trew that asshole bartenda an' all I hear is girls callin' out your name to come to the phone! How do ya think that makes me feel?!

FREDDIE. *(Tiredly.)* Oh man ... *(Beat.)* I'm workin' three nights a week.

DEBBIE. An' you're goin' to school for three nights!

FREDDIE. What have we got Debbie?! Huh? That radio an' Jess!

DEBBIE. I'm just sayin' you're goin' around doin' an' – an' I'm ... an' then you're on my back about everythin' I do! "Makeup's bad for the skin. Jeans are too tight. You should quit smokin'. You should go here an' go there an' do this an' do that!" But you didn't mind any a that in the tenth grade, did ya? You loved me in the park! You loved me at the Shipyard Drive-In! You loved me on my mother's couch!

FREDDIE. Whaddaya doin'?! What the fuck are you talkin' about?!

DEBBIE. I ... I want things back like before Freddie. I want me an' you to go to bed an' watch a TV movie an' I put my head on your shoulder an' hear the TV in my sleep an' feel you an' hear the TV at the same time. I never used ta be scared then. *(She hugs Freddie. He hugs her back. They remain motionless for a couple of beats.)*

FREDDIE. I just ... I don't know what ta say, I uh gotta get the van fixed an' ...

DEBBIE. It's always been you Freddie an' – an' when you start actin' like Mistah smarty-pants puttin' me an' Kathy Martin down ... I think you're gettin' ready to yunno take off on me, right, like my father did an' I freak, all right? I freak. *(Freddie moves away from her.)*

FREDDIE. Let's not get into this shit right now.

DEBBIE. I mean tanight I needed you there.

FREDDIE. Right, right.

DEBBIE. I really did Freddie.

FREDDIE. I play out in the band 'cause I ...

DEBBIE. You could do other things besides ...

FREDDIE. I do other things in the day but the band is somethin' that I ...

DEBBIE. Girls!

FREDDIE. We gonna go through this again?!

DEBBIE. Girls! Pawtucket girls! Woonsocket girls! Cranston girls! Warwick girls!

FREDDIE. You're pickin' up right where we left off, right?

DEBBIE. East Providence!

FREDDIE. Cut it out Debbie!

DEBBIE. You just don't admit to it! *(Freddie breaks. Steps to*

her with his hand raised ready to strike her.)
FREDDIE.   I said CUT IT OUT or I'm goin' to kick ya ass!
Put a fuckin' lid on it man! My fuckin' head is ringin' with
all kinds a shit an' listenin' to your – your same stupid rap is
makin' me nuts! *(Beat.)* When I left you to go to the club I'm
drivin' on Route Ten, van is smokin' front an' back, the radio don't work an' people drivin' by me are givin' me the finger, right? In my head all I hear is your voice "I don't care
nothin' about you! I hate your guts! Don't come back!"
DEBBIE.   Didn't stop you from leavin', did it?
FREDDIE.   An' I think "she shoulda married the Guinea in
Japan."
DEBBIE.   Oh please ...
FREDDIE.   Honest ta shit, man, this is what I'm thinkin'
when I notice I can't see much 'cause a the smoke an' I can't
see the exit, nothin'! Nothin' but smoke. Lookit my hands,
thinkin' about it got me shakin'! Lookit my hands ...
DEBBIE.   *(Dryly.)* I see 'em. They're shakin'.
FREDDIE.   They're shakin', right?
DEBBIE.   How come people were givin' you the finga?
FREDDIE.   'Cause of the smoke from the van.
DEBBIE.   *(Dryly.)* Fuckin' people.
FREDDIE.   Yeah an' I finally get off near Olneyville an' I'm
at that light there when these people get outta their cars an'
start yellin' at me. They're blamin' me for the – the hole
there, the ozone thing, yunno, blamin' me for puttin' a hole
in the earth!
DEBBIE.   You fuck! You was high!
FREDDIE.   No I wasn't, I ...
DEBBIE.   The smoke was comin' from inside the van, you
bastard!
FREDDIE.   It wasn't. I was straight tonight an' c'mon, you
know how much I hate it when we argue about dope.
DEBBIE.   Oh yeah ... "lost in Olneyville" with people bangin'
on the van sayin' "you're puttin' a hole in the earth." If I or
Kathy Martin said somethin' like that you'd have a shit-fit!
FREDDIE.   Forget it, just forget it, all right? I was just sayin'
you shoulda married that Guinea in Japan an' that's what I

74

was thinkin' when I was in the van when everythin' just uh, just went crazy.

DEBBIE. We'll see if that joint is still there. *(Freddie glares at Debbie. Pause.)*

FREDDIE. Why don't ya go check? Go ahead. Go down to the parkin' lot an' take a coupla hits, why don't ya? *(He gives Debbie a shove.)*

DEBBIE. Freddie?!

FREDDIE. Go get high Debbie an' we'll fuckin' talk. Go get your buzz on girl. Go ahead. *(He pushes Debbie again. Harder. She cocks back her fist.)*

DEBBIE. Don't you fuckin' push me!

FREDDIE. What happened again? Lemme get this straight so I know what they know.

DEBBIE. She fell down the cellar stairs 'cause you forgot to lock the stupid door an' I heard the noise like – like boxes fallin' or – or ... a box ... fallin' downstairs and I ran an' saw the door opened an' – an' put the light on an' there she was not movin' way at the bottom an' I ran down an' picked her up an' she was like ... I mean her arms an' her head just kinda fell back yunno like a dead pigeon from the road and I ...

INTERCOM. Mrs. Campbell, dial 8-3-1, Mrs. Campbell, dial 8-3-1.

DEBBIE. I hate her!

FREDDIE. Go get your buzz, I'll cover, right?

DEBBIE. What is your problem?!

FREDDIE. Go get high an' then we'll see Jess. Go on. Joint's in the ashtray.

DEBBIE. I'm gonna wait ...

FREDDIE. Shit, afta tonight an' what you been through you need a good buzz, don't ya think?

DEBBIE. I been through a lot.

FREDDIE. I know, I know.

DEBBIE. I hated bein' in the Rescue Squad.

FREDDIE. It sucks.

DEBBIE. You always hear the siren for someone else an' ...

FREDDIE. Then somethin' fucked up happens an' ...

DEBBIE. I mean you had the van.

FREDDIE. You had to call the Rescue.

DEBBIE. I had ta.

FREDDIE. Right afta she fell?

DEBBIE. What?

FREDDIE. When did you call?

DEBBIE. I don't ...

FREDDIE. Right afta she fell?

DEBBIE. It was ...

FREDDIE. Or right afta you hit her?

DEBBIE. What?

FREDDIE. When did you call?

DEBBIE. When she wouldn't come to.

FREDDIE. You fuckin' whacked her, didn't you?!

DEBBIE. Freddie?!

FREDDIE. You hit her!

DEBBIE. She fell down the ...

FREDDIE. LIE!

DEBBIE. NO!

FREDDIE. I SEEN HER! I BEEN HERE FOR AN HOUR! THEY TOOK ME UPSTAIRS!

DEBBIE. *(Stunned.)* She ... she fell down the ...

FREDDIE. You fuckin' lie about everythin'!

DEBBIE. I'm not ...

FREDDIE. You lie like most people tell the truth!

DEBBIE. Whaddaya mean you been here for an' hour?!

FREDDIE. When I got here they fuckin' hustled me upstairs, okay, an' they talked an' – an' the doctor an' nurse told me everything about you havin' a fit an' then ...

DEBBIE. You been here the whole time?!

FREDDIE. Shut up!

DEBBIE. An' you didn't come in here to see me?!

FREDDIE. They wanted to talk to me alone an' ... an' they took me to Jess an' I seen through some glass an' – an' she looked fine to me but then she ... they turned her over an' I ... I saw her whole face an' it was like it was divided, split in two an' one whole side was swollen an' ... *(Debbie turns away but Freddie grabs her and forces her to look him in the face.)* Her face was swollen an' black an' red an' – an' her eye was shut 'cause 'cause the swellin' was so fuckin' bad an' there was black stitches in the corner of her lip an' her ear was covered with a bandage an' they had wires glued to her hair an' hooked to a machine an' I ... I didn't know, I mean you couldn't tell it was Jess 'til they turned her back over an' the other side was ... that was Jess ... *(Debbie breaks from him.)*

DEBBIE.   Oh I don't FUCKIN' believe this!

FREDDIE.   You beat one side of her face an' I seen it an' it's not from fallin' down stairs!

DEBBIE.   Listen to me ... I ...

FREDDIE.   Just tell the goddamn truth Debbie! For once tell the truth. To these people we're nothing but garbage an' they see right through all this. An' I'm up there feelin' like a complete asshole and the doctor's talkin' to me about her head an' ...

DEBBIE.   Yeah from fallin' down the ...

FREDDIE.   YOUR HANDPRINT IS ON HER FACE! I SEEN IT!

DEBBIE.   Yeah right, probly from when I was takin' her to the sink an' was holdin' her head unda the water to uh ...

FREDDIE.   They go through this every day Debbie! Don't you understand it's time to stop?! They're tellin' me we could lose her, that the state could take her, the same way Kathy Martin lost her kids, okay? I mean, fuck! They're talkin' about police reports an' – an' how we gotta ...

DEBBIE.   I'm not afraid a that shit! Jess fell down the stairs afta opening up the wrong door to the ...

FREDDIE.   They got this lady comin' in from this Child Services, this Mrs. Campbell to ...

DEBBIE.   So what?!

FREDDIE.   So tell her the truth! Tell her you whacked Jess an' you'll never do it again!

DEBBIE.   *(A beat.)* Screw you an' the ship you came in on, man!

FREDDIE.   *(A beat.)* All right ... great. Fuckin' great. *(He picks up his coat. Debbie watches him.)*

DEBBIE.   What?

FREDDIE. Whaddaya mean "what?"

DEBBIE. Whaddaya doin'?

FREDDIE. I'm ...

DEBBIE. You're the husband. You're my husband.

FREDDIE. *(By the door.)* I'm tired of it Deb. The lies. Olney Street. Kathy Martin. The fires. The summer. The stupid van. Route Ten. The TV. I'm sick a bein' garbage an' *(Beat.)* I thought maybe if I could get you to tell the truth for once, yunno, but ... I'm goin' to go upstairs an' do it for you then there might be a chance of somethin' 'cause we're headed straight for a telephone pole, girl, fuckin' crash city if ...

DEBBIE. *(Moves to him.)* So when you go upstairs, whaddaya gonna tell 'em? That you never hit your kid? That you never got hit? An' I suppose none of the nurses hit their kids! C'mon, everybody hits their kids. Kids whine an' bitch, Freddie, an' hey I seen you whack Jess good on the ass for rippin' a page outta your school book that one time, right?

FREDDIE. *(Softly.)* Did you beat her?

DEBBIE. If I had a buck every time I got a backhanda but fuck who cares 'bout that an' now they make such a big deal 'cause some Jew-doctor writes a book an' gets on TV to say some bullshit that he knows nothin' about!

FREDDIE. Are you goin' to tell the truth?

DEBBIE. Everybody has heard what I've got ta say about it!

FREDDIE. You been lyin' since we been in school an' you lied about not carin' 'bout the Guinea in Japan an' you lied about takin' the pill an' you lied sayin' we could handle havin' a kid an' you lied when you an' Kathy Martin was doin' drugs an' tellin' me you wasn't!

DEBBIE. An' alot of the shit goin' down with us wouldn't be happenin' if you'd take that job at Colan Plastics an' you know it!

FREDDIE. I told you I'm not workin' in a factory like my Old Man did!

DEBBIE. Kathy can get you in.

FREDDIE. I don't want to talk on this right now!

DEBBIE. *(Gets closer to him.)* All the benefits an' we could have nights together, right? I just always wanted to be with you

an' not with Chris in Japan. *(She wraps herself around Freddie.)*
FREDDIE. Yeah, right.
DEBBIE. Why'd I go with you then?
FREDDIE. *(Proudly.)* 'Cause I made you, that's why.
DEBBIE. *(Beat.)* Don't leave me here alone ...
INTERCOM. Mrs. Campbell, dial 8-3-1, Mrs. Campbell, dial
8-3-1. *(Freddie moves away from Debbie. She stands alone.)*
DEBBIE. What are you goin' to do? *(Freddie takes a breath, stands motionless.)* I know you love me a lot, I know it, an' you should get that job at Colan Plastics. Kathy Martin says you'd do good in shippin' an' I just gotta see more of you Freddie. *(Beat.)* I spend alotta time just thinkin' about you an' that's not good, yunno, an' I'm holdin' Jess an' I'm spacin' out the winda to the Brewery an' – an' there was times with me an' Jess, yunno, at first, like her first merry-go-round ride at the Park an' me an' you holdin' her tight so she wouldn't be scared a fallin' an' ... I – I rememba that day an' ... *(She is fighting back tears.)* Now I got Jess but I don't feel her, right, 'cause I'm piturin' you at some table with a girl an' – an' I forget I got Jess an' then she'll like drop her pacifier or – or hit me an' I freak, right, I mean I feel like droppin' her an' at the same time I feel like a piece-of-shit for thinkin' that kinda stuff an' both things hittin' me at once an' if there's nothin' to put in the pipe I get more freaked then I think about bein' a mother an' all that comes to mind is my mother an' – an' I feel sick 'cause I ... an' then I freak on top of freak, yunno, I mean it's like everythin's on my head at once an' Jess is wantin' somethin' an' then I smell the club on you when you get in bed an' I can't sleep an' then it's mornin' again an' I'm countin' out soda cans to buy cigarettes an' here comes asshole Charlie to pick you up to go clean toilets for practically no money an' the band is a fuckin' dream you get to have an' do an' I don't know ... I don't know what I'm supposed to do ... *(Debbie is broken. Pause. Door opens. Enter Nurse Sue with two cans of soda. Debbie turns away to gather herself.)*
SUE. How we doin' in here? *(Nothing. She places the cans on the examining table. Moves to the sink to wash her hands.)* Soon as

we get Mrs. Campbell we can go upstairs, okay? *(Beat.)* Honey, don't smoke in here.

DEBBIE.   I'm not.

SUE.   You were.

DEBBIE.   I wasn't.

SUE.   Okay, okay.

DEBBIE.   You knew he was here the whole time, didn't you? *(Sue picks up the clipboard. Looks at Freddie.)*

SUE.   Listen you two ... some advice you can take or leave. When the people from Child Services get here, tell them what really happened, all right? Don't be ashamed. When they know something's not totally right, if they sense that there's a hole in your story, they're not going to play around. Jess will be put in the care of the state.

FREDDIE.   *(To Debbie.)* Do you hear what she's saying?

DEBBIE.   She fell down the stairs. *(Freddie takes a moment to look at Debbie. He takes a breath then looks to Sue.)*

FREDDIE.   Uh look, it's my fault for not lockin' that stupid door an' uh if the state don't buy that — that it was my mistake then uh shit yunno I understand they gotta do what they gotta do ...

SUE.   Uh-huh ... *(Silence. Debbie stares at Freddie.)*

FREDDIE.   *(To Sue.)* Shit ... I bet you're a good parent, huh?

DEBBIE.   She told me she has two girls.

FREDDIE.   Wow.

DEBBIE.   Two, right?

SUE.   Two.

DEBBIE.   One's plenty.

FREDDIE.   No boys?

SUE.   Just girls.

FREDDIE.   My mother had all boys. Six.

DEBBIE.   Imagine.

FREDDIE.   Six.

SUE.   *(Looks to Freddie.)* Maybe you need more time to think on this.

FREDDIE.   I don't need more time. *(Grabs a can of soda and opens it.)* Let's get it over with. *(He drinks. Sue leaves. Silence.)*

INTERCOM.   Doctor Bozzarra, please report to pediatrics.

Doctor Bozzarra to pediatrics. (*Silence. Freddie moves to the U.R. wall and leans up against it. Debbie is by the examining table.*)

DEBBIE. I was just thinkin' about when me an' you was first goin' out an' we were really the hot shits a school. Goin' to parties 'cause everybody wanted us there. Cruisin' ta Rocky Point before the Mustang started to smoke on us, heads out the windas an' smellin' the ocean, right? Rememba? The band doin' the gigs at C-Y-O dances an' me right up front nearest to you. God I haven't heard you guys in so long it's amazin'. How long has it been Freddie? When's the last time I heard you guys?

FREDDIE. (*Softly.*) I don't know ...

DEBBIE. Well it's been long, I know that. (*Pause. Freddie speaks softly.*)

FREDDIE. Every year my old man would get a dog an' it would stay for a while an' when it fucked up like shit on the floor or it barked too much he would take it for a ride to dump it. I went with him a coupla times ... and I'd watch him drive faster than the dog could run an' ... an' the next day, for some reason he always went back to look for the dog. He never found them an' a week or so later he uh ... he'd get another one.

DEBBIE. Why are you sayin' that?

FREDDIE. An' he always dropped 'em off on the same street an' I asked him once about that an' he said "habit."

DEBBIE. Freddie? Why are you ...

FREDDIE. (*Quickly.*) 'Cause I feel like it. (*Freddie removes a Walkman from his coat pocket and puts on the headset. Debbie turns on her radio and searches for a good song. Both are crying as lights fade to black.*)

END OF PLAY

PROPERTY LIST

Radio/tape player (DEBBIE)
Cigarette (DEBBIE)
Matches or lighter (DEBBIE)
Clipboard (SUE)
2 soda cans (SUE)
Walkman radio with earphones (FREDDIE)

SOUND EFFECTS

Noise from hospital corridor
Phone buzzer

NOTES

(Use this space to make notes for your production)